THE HEINZ DAYS OUT
WITH KIDS

1997/98

NORTH EAST
EDITION

To Dave, for his constant enthusiasm and support – and to Anna, Jack and Sam for coming, doing and enjoying all those days out!

THE HEINZ GUIDE TO DAYS OUT WITH KIDS

1997/98 *EDITION*

TRIED-AND-TESTED FUN FAMILY OUTINGS IN THE NORTH EAST

HELEN GORSKY

BON•BON
PUBLISHING

FIRST PUBLISHED IN 1997 BY
BON•BON PUBLISHING
24 ENDLESHAM ROAD
LONDON SW12 8JU

COPYRIGHT © BON•BON PUBLISHING 1997

COVER PHOTOGRAPHS:
FRONT COVER © 1995 COMSTOCK
BACK COVER SHOWS DUNSTANBURGH CASTLE, NORTHUMBERLAND © "ENGLISH HERITAGE PHOTOGRAPHIC LIBRARY"

The right of Helen Gorsky to be identified
as the author of this work has been asserted by her in
accordance with the Copyright, Designs and Patents Act 1988.

A catalogue record for this book is available from the
British Library.

All rights reserved. No part of this publication may be
reproduced, transmitted, or stored in a retrieval system,
in any form or by any means, without permission in
writing from the publishers.

Every effort has been made to ensure the accuracy of
information in this book. Details such as opening times
and prices are subject to change and the authors and
publishers cannot accept liability for any errors or
omissions.

ISBN   1-901411-07-9

SERIES EDITOR JANET BONTHRON
DESIGN BY CAROLINE GRIMSHAW
ILLUSTRATIONS BY SAM TOFT

PRINTED & BOUND BY
BIDDLES LTD,
GUILDFORD, SURREY

Dear Reader

Heinz is delighted once again to be involved with this guide, particularly as it has so quickly established itself as one of the most comprehensive and reliable of its type.

For millions of people Heinz conjures up warm, fond memories of childhood and the security of home. It's one of those brands which seems to play a central part in almost everyone's family life. That's why it is so appropriate that we should be sponsoring this guide which is devoted to making the most of life with your kids. I do hope you find it a useful source of reference.

Yours faithfully

JANE ST CLAIR-MILLER
HJ HEINZ COMPANY

More about

Henry John Heinz was little more than a kid himself when he established his food business. At the age of 16 he began to bottle dried and grated horseradish from the family garden of his home in Sharpsburg, Pennsylvania.

He packed his product in clear glass bottles so that his customers could see he was selling only horseradish - without bits of turnip or other cheap fillers that other people used. Although he could not have known it at the time, he was starting a venture which was to grow into one of the world's great food enterprises.

In 1886 the British got to sample Heinz products for the first time. Henry Heinz visited London with five cases of products and called on Fortnum and Mason, who promptly bought the lot. The first British factory was established in 1905 in Peckham and a custom-made factory was built at Harlesden in north London in the mid 1920s.

That factory still stands and is an important production centre, but it is dwarfed by the factory built in Kitt Green near Wigan in 1959, Europe's largest food factory. Today there are 360 Heinz products in the UK alone, ranging from well-known favourites like Heinz Baked Beans and Heinz Spaghetti through to all sorts of fun meal time treats like Thomas the Tank Engine pasta shapes, Heinz Baked Beans with Pork Sausages and Heinz Spaghetti Hoops with Hot Dogs.

HENRY J HEINZ

A history of Heinz

1844	Henry John Heinz born, Sharpsburg, Pennsylvania
1869	HJ Heinz Company formed
1886	Heinz Tomato Ketchup sold in Fortnum & Mason
1895	Heinz Baked Beans first sold
1910	Cream of Tomato Soup first sold in the UK
1925	Spaghetti added to the company's range
1938	Heinz Baby Food first sold
1946	Heinz Tomato Ketchup first manufactured in UK
1959	Kitt Green factory opened, Europe's largest food factory
1995	Heinz celebrates 100 years of Heinz Baked Beans
1996	Heinz celebrates 100 years of "57 Varieties"

The magic number "57"

In 1896 Henry Heinz spotted a shoe advertisement which read "21 styles". That set him totting up his own products; 56, 57, 58, 59... There were still a few more, but something made him linger on "57". It seemed a distinctive number, so "57 Varieties" it was. Today the worldwide business markets many hundreds of products under various brand names, but the famous "57 Varieties" trademark has passed into the language.

Contents

Introduction	**5**
How To Use This Book	**7**
Map	**10**
Planning Guide	**12**

Animal Encounters

Bill Quay Farm	**15**
Hall Hill Farm	**18**
Jedforest Deer & Farm Park	**21**
Marlish Farm	**24**
Newham Grange Farm	**27**

Look! Look! Look!

Butterfly World & Preston Hall Museum	**30**
Hancock Museum	**33**
Killhope Leadmining Centre	**36**
National Railway Museum	**39**
Newcastle Discovery Museum	**42**
Tynemouth Sea Life Centre	**45**
Washington Wildfowl & Wetland Centre	**48**
Woodhorn Colliery Museum	**51**

The Great Outdoors

Bellingham	**54**
Belsay Hall	**57**
Cragside Country Park	**60**
The Farne Islands	**63**
Hardwick Hall	**66**
The Leas & Marsden Rock	**69**
Nature's World	**72**
Newby Hall	**75**
Thornley Wood	**78**
Wallington Hall	**81**

Somewhat Historical

Alnwick Castle	**84**
Bamburgh Castle	**87**
Beamish Museum	**90**
Bede's World	**93**
Durham Cathedral	**96**
Hartlepool Historic Quay	**99**
Housesteads Fort & Hadrian's Wall	**102**
Richmond Castle & Town	**105**
Warkworth Castle	**108**

Up, Down, There & Back

Heatherslaw Railway	**111**
South Tynedale Railway	**114**
Tanfield Railway	**117**

The Sun Has Got His Hat On

Allen Banks & Plankey Mill	**120**
Bolam Lake	**123**
Bowlees	**126**
Dunstanburgh	**129**
Finchale Priory	**132**

Introduction

WELCOME TO THE HEINZ GUIDE TO DAYS OUT WITH KIDS, A BOOK written for people with children in the North East. Here in its second edition, it is packed with ideas for fun family outings. With new outings to try and revised information on all other trips, I hope that it will continue to help you tackle some of those perennial problems:

WHAT ARE WE GOING TO DO TODAY?
As a mother of three children, I know how important it is to get out of the house some days. Equally, how difficult it can be to think of places to go for a change; places that are not too far; where everyone can have a good time; where young children will be well catered for. This book gives you a personal selection of great outings to choose from; if you go out on one or two a month, there are well over a year's worth of different trips inside!

BUT WHERE IS REALLY GOOD?
Often these days it is not a problem knowing about places to go, but rather whether those places will really be a good trip for people with children. If you've no time to sift through leaflets, or don't know anyone who's been themselves then it can be daunting to try something new. The outings featured in The Heinz Guide to Days Out With Kids have all been done personally, by mothers with children in tow. They are all tried-and-tested recommended trips: we've been there ourselves!

WHAT ABOUT MUMS AND DADS TOO?
If the prospect of yet another adventure playground bores you, then you'll welcome something different. Our aim has been to describe outings enjoyed by everyone in the family, with something to appeal to adults as well as children. Some of the trips may look like just adult outings, but they're not. We want to introduce you to some of the unusual and fun places we have been to. You may all get something different out of the day, but that doesn't matter, as long as you all have a good time.

How Are Places Selected For The Book?
We have included a variety of trips: for the winter and the summer, for rain and sunshine, some nearby, some a greater distance. Some of the trips are old favourites, many times visited. Others were suggested by friends as places that they love. We have noted what childcare facilities are provided in each case: pushchair accessibility, high chairs, nappy tables etc., but haven't selected places purely on this basis. Rather, the facilities information is given on the principle that if you know in advance what is provided you can plan your day accordingly.

All trips were done anonymously. No one has paid to be included in the book, and the views and opinions expressed are very much personal thoughts and reactions. Places are in the book because we had a good time there, and think that other people with children could too.

What Ages Of Children Are Covered?
The book is aimed at people with babies, toddlers and school-aged children. Many of the trips will also appeal to children up to early teens, and, of course, adults too!

The facts given for each outing have been checked rigorously. However, things do change, and please check details (particularly opening times) before you set out.

Finally, we'd love to receive your comments on any of the places you visit from this book. Also any of your ideas on places we could include in the next edition. The ten best suggestions we are sent will receive a copy of the new edition absolutely free. Please send them to me at the address below.

Janet Bonthron
Series Editor
**Bon•Bon Ventures
24 Endlesham Road
London SW12 8JU**

How To Use This Book

EACH SECTION OF THE BOOK COVERS TRIPS WHICH FALL INTO THE same broad category of attraction. Outings are described alphabetically within the section. If you know what sort of outing you want to do, then just look at the section titles, read the section summaries below, and flick through the entries included in that section. Alternatively, the handy planning guide is a rapid, self-explanatory table for identifying the right trip for you.

ANIMAL ENCOUNTERS covers trips to farms, zoos and other birds and beasties type places. Children and animals are a winning combination, and there are plenty of places around the North East which offer it. We have chosen those which we think are distinctive in some way, for example superb handling opportunities for children, wonderful setting, or unusual or imaginatively-displayed animals. Try them all for variety!

LOOK! LOOK! LOOK! features places with exhibitions or displays which children should particularly enjoy, be they of old mining works (Killhope or Woodhorn), a natural history museum (Hancock Museum), or nose-to-nose contact with deep-sea creatures (Sea Life Centre). These outings offer the chance for children to see something unusual or to experience at close quarters something they may only have seen on television.

THE GREAT OUTDOORS is about trips which are all or mostly outdoors in character, in an especially beautiful or quiet setting. Ideal for walks and strolls, with plenty to see for adults whilst the little horrors run around exhausting themselves. Couldn't be better!

SOMEWHAT HISTORICAL attractions all have a bygone age theme. Your children may not fully appreciate the historical connotations, but will be able to enjoy the setting and exhibits, whilst you can wallow in romantic nostalgia!

UP, DOWN, THERE & BACK has steam train and canal ride outings. Puffs of steam and the smell of smoke in the air are always thrilling and the ones we have included have features which make them particularly accessible. Eat your heart out, Thomas the Tank Engine!

THE SUN HAS GOT HIS HAT ON includes picnic spots that are obviously just a small selection of what is available. Most good picnic spots tend to be closely guarded secrets, but these are ones which are favourites of ours. There is something about spreading your blanket on the ground and unpacking boxes and plates of picnic food that is just pure summertime, and you can't beat it. Happy munching! Of course, many of the locations in the previous sections are also excellent picnic spots.

If you don't mind what sort of attraction you go to, but have other criteria (such as the weather, distance, or means of transport for example) which you need to satisfy, then the best way to use the book is to refer to the map and planning guide given on the following pages. These should help you to pick a suitable day out.

THE PLANNING GUIDE can help you select an outing by distance, prevailing weather, admittance to dogs, accessibility by public transport, or opening hours.
* Free, or particularly good value, trips are asterisked (less than about £7.50 for a family of four).

Distances are approximate, and taken from Newcastle. We have erred on the generous side when deciding on the **wet weather** suitability – if there is somewhere to duck inside during an occasional shower then we say 'yes' under the wet weather trip heading. 'No' means, in our view, it would really be quite a miserable trip if it is raining. For people with **dogs**, 'yes' may mean on a lead only, so always take a lead.

With **public transport** accessibility we have indicated what is available, but you may need to do a short walk too in some cases. 'None' or 'limited' means that it would really be hard work going there without a car.

The planning guide also indicates whether **opening** periods are restricted (i.e. if a place is not open all the year, and/or only on some days of the week). For attractions cited as 'all year' opening, this excludes Christmas Day, Boxing Day and New Year's Day, so check if you want to go these days.

Once you have identified a trip that sounds appealing, refer to the detailed description for further information. Page numbers are given in the Planning Guide. The Fact File which accompanies each entry gives the address and telephone number, travel directions and distances, opening times and prices, and an indication of specific facilities (high chairs, nappy change areas and eating places). Where appropriate, the Fact File also suggests other nearby attractions.

Map

ANIMAL ENCOUNTERS	PAGE
1 Bill Quay Farm	15
2 Hall Hill Farm	18
3 Jedforest Deer & Farm Park	21
4 Marlish Farm	24
5 Newham Grange Farm	27

LOOK! LOOK! LOOK!

6 Butterfly World & Preston Hall Museum	30
7 Hancock Museum	33
8 Killhope Leadmining Centre	36
9 National Railway Museum	39
10 Newcastle Discovery Museum	42
11 Tynemouth Sea Life Centre	45
12 Washington Wildfowl & Wetland Centre	48
13 Woodhorn Colliery Museum	51

THE GREAT OUTDOORS

14 Bellingham	54
15 Belsay Hall	57
16 Cragside Country Park	60
17 The Farne Islands	63
18 Hardwick Hall	66
19 The Leas & Marsden Rock	69
20 Nature's World	72
21 Newby Hall	75
22 Thornley Wood	78
23 Wallington Hall	81

SOMEWHAT HISTORICAL	PAGE
24 Alnwick Castle	84
25 Bamburgh Castle	87
26 Beamish Museum	90
27 Bede's World	93
28 Durham Cathedral	96
29 Hartlepool Historic Quay	99
30 Housesteads Fort & Hadrian's Wall	102
31 Richmond Castle & Town	105
32 Warkworth Castle	108

UP, DOWN, THERE AND BACK

33 Heatherslaw Railway	111
34 South Tynedale Railway	114
35 Tanfield Railway	117

THE SUN HAS GOT HIS HAT ON

36 Allen Banks & Plankey Mill	120
37 Bolam Lake	123
38 Bowlees	126
39 Dunstanburgh	129
40 Finchale Priory	132

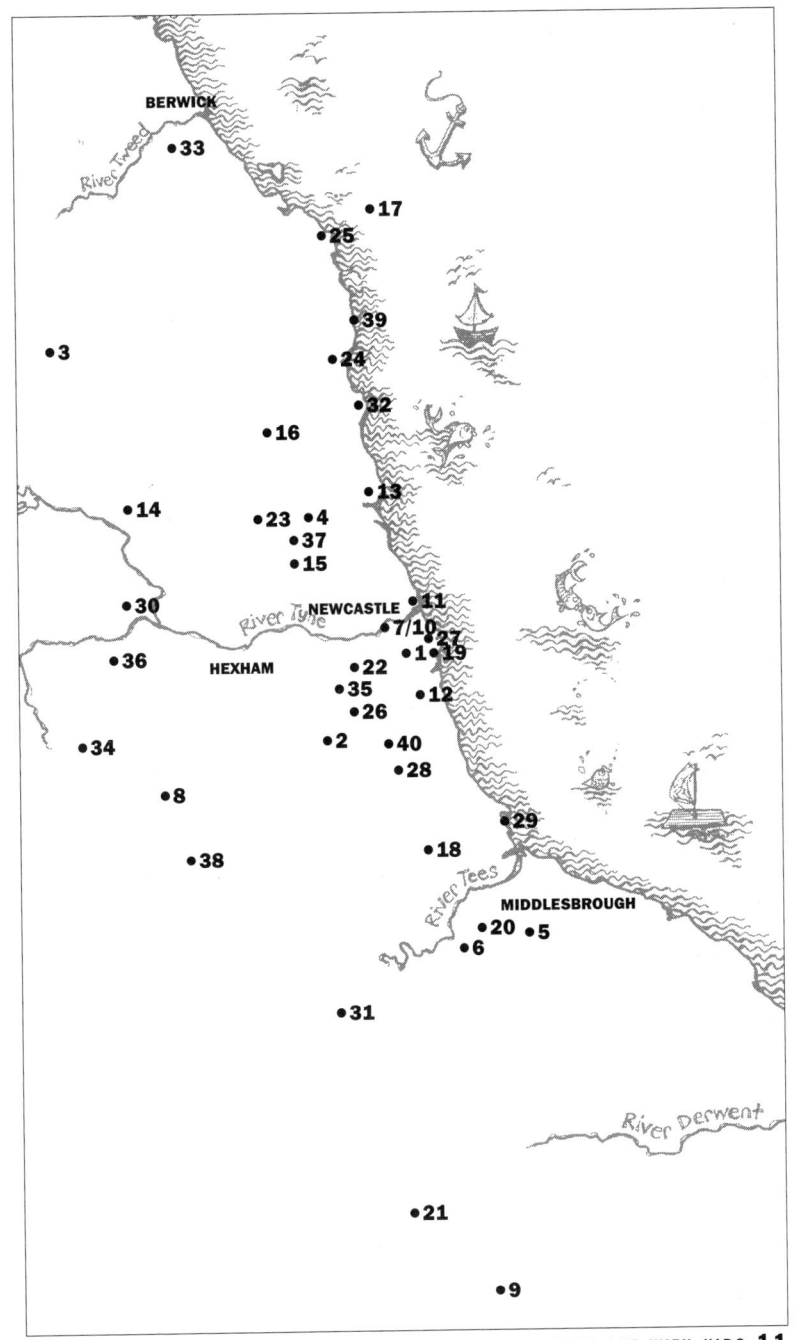

HEINZ GUIDE TO DAYS OUT WITH KIDS 11

Planning Guide

OUTING	DISTANCE (MILES)	WET WEATHER TRIP	DOGS	PUBLIC TRANSPORT	OPEN	PAGE
ANIMAL ENCOUNTERS						
Bill Quay Farm*	5	NO	YES	METRO	ALL YEAR	15
Hall Hill Farm	20	YES	NO	LIMITED	RESTRICTED	18
Jedforest Deer & Farm Park	55	YES	YES	BUS	RESTRICTED	21
Marlish Farm	22	NO	NO	NONE	RESTRICTED	24
Newham Grange Farm*	45	NO	NO	BUS	RESTRICTED	27
LOOK! LOOK! LOOK!						
Butterfly World & Preston Hall Museum	45	YES	NO	BUS	ALL YEAR	30
Hancock Museum*	0	YES	NO	YES	ALL YEAR	33
Killhope Leadmining Centre*	50	YES	YES	LIMITED	ALL YEAR	36
National Railway Museum	80	YES	NO	YES	ALL YEAR	39
Newcastle Discovery Museum*	0	YES	NO	YES	ALL YEAR	42
Tynemouth Sea Life Centre	7	YES	NO	METRO	ALL YEAR	45
Washington Wildfowl & Wetland Centre	15	YES	NO	BUS	ALL YEAR	48
Woodhorn Colliery Museum*	20	YES	NO	BUS	RESTRICTED	51
THE GREAT OUTDOORS						
Bellingham*	30	NO	YES	LIMITED	ALL YEAR	54
Belsay Hall	14	YES	YES	BUS	ALL YEAR	57
Cragside Country Park	30	NO	YES	BUS	RESTRICTED	60
The Farne Islands	50	NO	NO	BUS	RESTRICTED	63
Hardwick Hall*	30	NO	YES	BUS	ALL YEAR	66
The Leas & Marsden Rock*	25	NO	YES	METRO	ALL YEAR	69
Nature's World*	40	NO	NO	BUS	ALL YEAR	72
Newby Hall	75	NO	NO	BUS	RESTRICTED	75
Thornley Wood*	5	NO	YES	BUS	ALL YEAR	78
Wallington Hall	20	NO	YES	LIMITED	ALL YEAR	81

OUTING	DISTANCE (MILES)	WET WEATHER TRIP	DOGS	PUBLIC TRANSPORT	OPEN	PAGE
SOMEWHAT HISTORICAL						
Alnwick Castle	31	YES	NO	BUS	RESTRICTED	84
Bamburgh Castle	50	YES	NO	BUS	RESTRICTED	87
Beamish Museum	10	YES	NO	BUS	RESTRICTED	90
Bede's World*	10	YES	YES	METRO	RESTRICTED	93
Durham Cathedral*	20	YES	NO	YES	ALL YEAR	96
Hartlepool Historic Quay	35	YES	NO	BUS	ALL YEAR	99
Housesteads Fort & Hadrian's Wall*	35	NO	YES	LIMITED	ALL YEAR	102
Richmond Castle & Town*	50	NO	YES	BUS	ALL YEAR	105
Warkworth Castle*	31	NO	YES	BUS	ALL YEAR	108
UP, DOWN, THERE AND BACK						
Heatherslaw Railway	65	YES	YES	LIMITED	RESTRICTED	111
South Tynedale Railway*	40	YES	YES	BUS	RESTRICTED	114
Tanfield Railway	8	YES	YES	BUS	RESTRICTED	117
THE SUN HAS GOT HIS HAT ON						
Allen Banks & Plankey Mill*	30	NO	YES	BUS	ALL YEAR	120
Bolam Lake*	18	NO	YES	BUS	ALL YEAR	123
Bowlees*	58	NO	YES	LIMITED	ALL YEAR	126
Dunstanburgh*	32	NO	YES	BUS	RESTRICTED	129
Finchale Priory*	15	NO	YES	BUS	RESTRICTED	132

SEE **HOW TO USE THIS GUIDE** FOR EXPLANATIONS

Animal Encounters

Bill Quay Farm

THIS IS A SMALL, IMAGINATIVELY SET OUT CITY FARM IN GATESHEAD. The animals are accessible to young children and the artwork and climbable sculptures around the farm lift it beyond the realms of the ordinary. Built above the river opposite the Wallsend shipyards (with tremendous views of the giant cranes) it consists of two farmyards and two large barns set amidst well-landscaped fields and a wooded area. It is worth a visit simply to experience the feeling that somehow in the middle of the noisy city, there you are, wandering up a quiet country lane amongst rolling green fields.

> "The teams of squealing gingery piglets were a big hit"

All the farmyard favourites are here. There are sheep in the large field as you walk into the farm and a large pig pen under the trees. Turkeys, geese and ducks strut around the yard and a peacock and his wife shriek and scream as they wander inside and out. We were lucky and caught a glimpse of the male with his tail fully opened, which raised "oohs" and "aahs" from everyone and frantic pointing from the baby.

There is a short path taking you down between the fields so everyone can get a good look at the cows, ponies, sheep and goats. The latter are two very fine specimens with enormous horns certainly worthy of the Big Billy Goat Gruff. Their portraits ingeniously sculpted from scrap metal are set up on a wall nearby. Elsewhere on the farm there is a flock of wooden sheep, a line of wooden pigs, a giant wooden spider, a snake and a field of mammoth wooden corn stalks, all of which can be clambered on. For a longer walk right down to the riverside (passable for a pushchair) ask for directions at the farm office.

The animals inside the barn vary according to the season. We saw two sows that had recently farrowed and the teams of squealing gingery piglets were a big hit with the children. There are Jacobs sheep and Angora goats as well as other pigs, chicks and ducklings. There are also rabbits and guinea pigs in hutches. Although children can't handle the animals, many are friendly and can be patted and stroked over the bars. All the animals have names clearly marked above their pens and there is plenty of information about them which you can pass on.

Outside again there is a large picnic area and a giant chicken slide. This is the only playground item so it could get very crowded on a busy day. The cafe is open at weekends only, selling snacks, and there are also a couple of drinks vending machines. However there are plenty of picnic benches so bring your sandwiches and enjoy the view down the river while you eat.

The farm sells its own honey, eggs and goats milk. There is a lively programme of events usually in the school holidays; mostly crafts and environmentally-based, these tend to be spontaneous so check in advance. Other planned events this year include traditional Easter games and music on Easter Monday and a Halloween Spooks evening.

Fact File

- ADDRESS Hainingwood Terrace, Bill Quay, Gateshead, Tyne & Wear
- TELEPHONE 0191 438 5340
- DIRECTIONS Across the Tyne Bridge take A6115 to Felling. At the roundabout take A185 towards Hebburn, turn left up Station Road, Hainingwood Terrace is the second left turn
- PUBLIC TRANSPORT Take the Metro to Pelaw, turn left out of the station and walk down to the main road, cross and walk down Fisherwell Road. At the bottom turn right down a bridle way, this leads you to the farm (a 10-minute walk)
- DISTANCE 5 miles
- TRAVEL TIME 15 minutes
- OPENING 9.00am-5.00pm all year
- PRICES Free (donation box)
- RESTAURANT FACILITIES Limited
- NAPPY CHANGING FACILITIES Yes
- HIGH CHAIRS No
- DOGS Yes
- PUSHCHAIR-FRIENDLY Yes
- NEARBY Arbeia Roman Fort Museum, South Shields (0191 456 1369)

Hall Hill Farm

With a moo, moo here and a moo, moo there

Hall Hill is a well-organised farm set on the top of a steep hill in County Durham. All Old Macdonald's friends are here and everyone can ride in a farmyard trailer pulled by a tractor. For tractor fans this is a definite highlight. It also means you can visit outlying fields, where there are other animals and a riverside walk. If you choose a fine day (it is exposed and extremely chilly when windy), and come with a picnic, there is plenty at Hall Hill to keep the family busy all day.

In the farmyard there is a lively population of birds: peacocks, chickens, Rambo the cockerel and some ducks on a pond. Bags of food are on sale at the entrance (10p) for feeding the birds, sheep and goats. When we were there in the summer we watched as a cow in the farmyard was milked. Our three-year-old was so fascinated by this it started him off on a chain of questions about the origins of food. ("Where do baked beans grow? Where do sausages come from?") There are more cows and pigs to look at in one of the barns. On our visit there were also chicks which we could pick up and cuddle: a very special moment for all the kids.

> **"On our visit there were chicks which we could pick up and cuddle"**

There are paths around the farm leading alongside fields with deer and Highland cattle. The track is gravel in parts and can be hard work with a buggy. The adventure playground is excellent, though not suitable for under-2's. It has a circuit to do, stepping along tree stumps, across a wobbly bridge and so on. A picnic area adjoins the playground, so you can sit and watch while they play.

If it is wet there is a barn set aside for indoor picnics with hay bales to sit on. When you first arrive at the farm, everyone is handed a single cleansing wipe in a packet to use before eating. There are also notices everywhere reminding you to wash your hands after touching the animals – a helpful touch we thought.

When you can tear them away from the playground take the trailer ride up to the rest of the farm. This leaves hourly and takes about 10 minutes. Once there you have about half an hour to wander around looking at the animals. We saw llamas, sheep and a Shetland pony. There is a riverside walk open in the summer, but this begins with a very steep bank and notices advise pregnant women and very young children not to attempt it.

Back at the main part of the farm you can visit the tearoom and shop. If it is fine you can sit outside in the courtyard and there are some child-sized tables and chairs as well as several highchairs.

If you visit Hall Hill in spring you will see the newborn lambs and calves. At the end of May there is sheep shearing to watch. There are other special events too, such as a Teddy Bear Picnic and winter visits to see the animals in their stables, sing carols and meet Santa.

Fact File

- ADDRESS Hall Hill Farm, Lanchester, County Durham
- TELEPHONE 01388 730300
- DIRECTIONS Take the A692 from Newcastle towards Consett, and turn left onto the A6076 to Lanchester. From the town centre take the B6296, the farm is beyond Holinsdale
- PUBLIC TRANSPORT Stanley taxis Ruralride number 764 to farm gate. Weekdays only
- DISTANCE 20 miles
- TRAVEL TIME 40 minutes
- OPENING Sunday-Friday 1.30pm-5.00pm from 23 March to end August. Open at 10.30am Sundays and school holidays. Sundays only in September and October, plus daily 19-24 October
- PRICES Adults £3.00, children £2.00, under-3's free
- RESTAURANT FACILITIES Yes
- NAPPY CHANGING FACILITIES Yes
- HIGH CHAIRS Yes
- DOGS No
- PUSHCHAIR-FRIENDLY Yes
- NEARBY Malton Picnic area and Lanchester Valley walk, a wooded area with riverside walks

Jedforest Deer & Farm Park

JEDFOREST FARM IS WAY OUT IN THE HILLS OF THE BORDER COUNTRY A few miles into Scotland. Though a fair hike, it is well worth the trip, with plenty to keep you busy all day. You can even go on a drizzly day so long as you take wellies and anoraks, as the animals are still out and about and there is a wonderful barn to play in. It is a working farm with arable land, sheep, cows and a commercial herd of red deer. Tourism is its newest enterprise and it has been well set-out with thought to the needs of children with their short legs and short attention spans. Check out in advance the programme of on-going activities with a ranger – walks, mini-beast hunts and the like.

There are three play areas around the park, feeding and handling opportunities and various walks. You can picnic inside or out and if you're there on a fine day you might like to have a barbecue on one of the gas barbecues provided in the picnic area. Come with your own food (50p to use the barbecue) or be

"Many of the animals are tame and will hurry over to the fence as you approach"

adventurous and try a farm pack of venison burgers and sausages (£4.50 with rolls and ketchup included).

As you arrive, ignore the barn with 'feely' boxes inside (until the way back when the children have seen some animals). Head instead for the shop to buy tickets and cups of animal food (25p), and go straight into the rare breeds farm park. You can hire wellies here too before tramping off (25p). The animals are all in irregular shaped fields, often with paths along two sides for greater visibility. Many of the animals are tame and will hurry over to the fence as you approach. Beware of Hannibal the llama, he can spit from a range of about a metre: our toddler in the backpack got a shower! There are Highland cattle, Red Poll cattle and Belted Galloways with large white belts of hair around their bellies; also goats, poultry and a number of different breeds of sheep and pigs. Snuffly pigs always please our children and the goats here were popular too, particularly a small black billy who scrambled under gates and in and out of the fields as he chose.

One field (the Clapping Corner) is specifically for children to go inside to feed and pet the animals: there are rabbits and guinea pigs in runs as well as sheep, goats and a calf. These animals will nose and push at you for food. There is a duck pond too with a large identification board.

Once you've exhausted the rare breeds park there are two walks: the brown walk takes an hour and a half and goes out to the fishing lakes, whilst the green walk is about 30 minutes and gives you a good look at the deer. The

deer are beautiful – leggy fawns with Bambi eyes, shy females and elegant males standing poised under enormous antlers. If you visit in May or June you will see the fawns in their earliest days. You can take a buggy on this walk, but it would be hard going after heavy rain.

In the wood at the end of both walks is an excellent adventure playground with ropes, logs, bridges and tyres to climb and a tall covered slide. Great fun for five-year-olds and over but rather too large for younger ones. Another play area in the picnic field may suit little ones better, or head for the barn in the farmyard where there are kiddy tractors, a boat, puzzles, a tyre swing, a real tractor and hay bales to climb on and slide down – fun for all ages, parents included.

The self-service cafe offers snacks and drinks and there are ices in the shop. The shop has gifts, cards, and books. You can buy venison there too, in various different cuts with advice on the packs about how to cook it.

Fact File

- ADDRESS Jedforest Deer & Farm Park, Mervinslaw Estate, Camptown, Jedburgh
- TELEPHONE 01835 840364
- DIRECTIONS A696 onto the A68. Signposted from just beyond Camptown
- PUBLIC TRANSPORT Bus information from Newcastle Tourist Information (0191 261 0610)
- DISTANCE 55 miles
- TRAVEL TIME 1 hour 15 minutes
- OPENING Daily 10.00am-5.30pm May to end September, 11.00am-4.30pm October
- PRICES Adults £3.00, children £1.85, under-3's free. Family ticket £9.00
- RESTAURANT FACILITIES Yes
- NAPPY CHANGING FACILITIES Yes
- HIGH CHAIRS Yes
- DOGS Yes
- PUSHCHAIR-FRIENDLY Yes
- NEARBY Floors Castle, Kelso (01573 223333), for antiques collection and extensive grounds

Marlish Farm

MARLISH FARM IN THE HEART OF THE NORTHUMBRIAN COUNTRYSIDE IS well-established and popular within the area. The animals are used to being petted and stroked and will amble over to the edge of their enclosures as soon as they see people coming. Children are encouraged to offer them food from their hands and are invited to cuddle the rabbits, chicks and ducklings. In the spring the farm keeps as many pet lambs as it can and if you visit then you can help with bottle feeding and can hold the lambs and kids. The delight of our toddler at feeling the rough tongue of a calf on his palm and the excitement of our five-year-old at hugging a newborn lamb make Marlish a firm favourite and one of the places we visit again and again.

As you pay your entrance fee each child is given a big bag of food which can be offered to any animal along the way. They are warned not to hold their hands out to the pigs though! Be sure they keep a firm hold of their bag or even keep it in a pocket, since the goats particularly are greedy and given a chance will scoff the lot – including the bag.

> **"The excitement of our five-year-old at hugging a newborn lamb makes Marlish a firm favourite"**

In the enclosures there are sheep, goats, cows, ponies and pigs. There are some different breeds including Jacobs sheep and Vietnamese pot-bellied pigs, whose snub-nosed piglets always draw squeals from the children. Chickens and ducks wander freely and in the barns you may find baby chicks and ducklings or even kittens.

Spring is the time to see the very young calves, kids and lambs (although you should avoid it at this time if you are pregnant). The expectant ewes and new mothers and babies are kept in a large plastic tunnel and you can admire the white lambs on their wobbly legs and sympathise with the pregnant ewes as they huff and puff and wait. You may even be lucky enough to see a lamb being born, an unforgettable experience for children that will lift their visit into the realms of the extraordinary and will give them all sorts of questions for you to field on the way home. In a barn next door the lambs that need to be hand-fed are kept. This is the place to head for a turn at bottle-feeding (look for a notice or ask at the entrance for times).

Don't plan on eating here unless you bring your own food, there are a couple of drinks machines but nothing more substantial. If you bring a picnic there is a pleasant grassy area where you can sit, or if it's chilly you can go into the teaching area in one of the barns and sit at the school tables and chairs. There is a fabulous collection of old tractors standing around the farm for children to play on.

If you fancy walking further afield, follow the track down to the quarry marked by the red arrows. This is being developed as a wildlife walk to encourage children to enjoy the countryside and take notice of the insects and birds as well as the farmyard animals. There is a longer walk too, a 90-minute round trip that takes you down to the river and along the bank. This is marked by the blue arrows.

Back at the farmyard the shop has a good selection of farm animals and picture postcards of animals, all at pocket money prices. One last point, Marlish Farm is in the heart of the countryside and it can be pretty chilly and windswept out there in spring and autumn, so come prepared to wrap up warmly.

Fact File

- ADDRESS Marlish Farm, Hartburn, Morpeth, Northumberland
- TELEPHONE 01670 772223
- DIRECTIONS The A696 from Newcastle. Right turn beyond Belsay to Bolam Lake, and follow signs to Marlish Farm
- PUBLIC TRANSPORT None
- DISTANCE 22 miles
- TRAVEL TIME 40 minutes
- OPENING Daily 14 February to October, 10.00am-5.00pm
- PRICES Adult £2.50, child £1.75, under-2's free
- RESTAURANT FACILITIES No
- NAPPY CHANGING FACILITIES No
- HIGH CHAIRS No
- DOGS No
- PUSHCHAIR-FRIENDLY Yes
- NEARBY Shaftoe Crags

Newham Grange Farm

Newham Grange is a small friendly farm on the outskirts of Middlesbrough. It is well set-up for animal lovers with highly accessible enclosures, opportunities to cuddle and feed their favourites and a great play area. For parents and older children there are several 19th century rooms to look at and a large display of vintage farm machinery.

It is a working farm and has a stock of rare breeds including several breeds of pig, such as the Tamworth, Gloucester Old Spot, Berkshire, Saddleback and Large White. These vast creatures with their grunty snouts and muddy trotters always seem to delight children and the pig units provide a good chance to see them at close quarters and to admire the litters of piglets. Elsewhere on the farm there are donkeys, ponies, sheep, cows and goats, all tame and well-used to children. You can buy bags of food at the shop (20p) and the sheep and goats will eat from an outstretched hand, but be careful as they don't always wait to be offered and will have a nibble at the bag too if they can. There is a small pond with ducks and geese and also plenty of chickens, turkeys and a peacock around. The small hatchery has an incubator inside and when we went the children were able to hold the chicks, which they loved. There are also lots of guinea pigs, some of them for sale.

Interspersed with the animal pens are the period rooms: a reproduction of an agricultural merchant's shop, a 19th century vet's surgery and a saddler's shop, which all provide good talking points with children. The Visitors' Centre tells the story of the farm from the 17th century to the present day in words and pictures. There is a lovely display of old equipment in a Victorian kitchen too, but this is up a steep flight of steps and is well above toddler eye level.

The play area has a variety of swings, slide, bouncy animals and a tractor climbing

"The vast pigs with their grunty snouts and muddy trotters always seem to delight children"

28 HEINZ GUIDE TO DAYS OUT WITH KIDS

frame. It is next to a field where you can picnic or there is a small cafe serving sandwiches, cakes and drinks and a few hot meals for children (oen most Sundays and Bank Holidays). You can buy ices and drinks at the shop which also sells cards and toy animals.

Since it is a working farm if you time your visit right you can watch lambing, sheep dipping or shearing. There may be a chance to help bottlefeed the lambs, cuddle a piglet or even have a go at milking the goat. Various events are arranged throughout the summer months, including bird-box building, beekeeping, walking-stick-making, a blacksmith demonstration and a children's fun day (phone for details). On the day we went there was a scarecrow-making afternoon which was very popular, older and younger kids having a whale of a time stuffing straw into old clothes, making hats and drawing faces on sacks. The finished scarecrows were to be saved for the Hallowe'en walk!

Fact File

- ADDRESS Newham Grange Leisure Farm, Wykeham Way, Coulby Newham, Middlesbrough, Cleveland
- TELEPHONE 01642 300261
- DIRECTIONS Turn off the A19 onto the A174 towards Whitby and Teesport. Turn right onto the A172, then right at roundabout. Follow signs to farm
- PUBLIC TRANSPORT Bus from Middlesbrough to Coulby Newham (01642 262626)
- DISTANCE 45 miles
- TRAVEL TIME 1 hour
- OPENING Daily in summer 9.30am-5.30pm. Weekends only in winter 10.00am-4.00pm. Last admission one hour before closing
- PRICES Adults £1.50, children 75p, under-3's free, family £4.00
- RESTAURANT FACILITIES Yes
- NAPPY CHANGING FACILITIES Yes
- HIGH CHAIRS Yes
- DOGS No
- PUSHCHAIR-FRIENDLY Yes
- NEARBY Saltburn for cliff tramway and Smugglers Heritage Centre (01287 625252)

Look! Look! Look!

Butterfly World & Preston Hall Museum

ON ONE OF THOSE BLEAK NORTHERN DAYS WITH A BITING WIND, TAKE yourselves off to the tropics in Butterfly World. Step through the door into a lush steamy rain forest, stroll amongst banana trees and giant palms and watch hundreds of exotic butterflies darting amongst the flowers. The feeling of warmth, the glimpses of colour – scarlet, turquoise, yellow, dusty blue – the splashing waterfall and the pools, all delight children and may even carry you to another world.

> "A large black and crimson butterfly uncurled itself and seemed to flicker into life"

Butterfly World is set in an extensive greenhouse, filled with tropical trees and plants. The butterflies fly about quite freely and will alight on flowers so close by that even a baby notices them. Our one-year-old squealed and pointed frantically from his buggy while the older two children were thrilled by the fact that they could spot as many as we could, their size for once being an advantage as they peered into the undergrowth and looked at the underside of leaves. A path winds amongst the trees past pools, a waterfall and a clearing where fruit is set out to tempt the butterflies enabling you to observe them feeding. There is a huge number of species, varying in size, wing shape, pattern and colour. Some birds also live in the greenhouse and their calls make it seem even more jungle-like. One pool is full of large Koi fish with gaping mouths which can be fed with bags of food from the shop.

At one end of the house there is an emerging cabinet hung with pupae and we watched enthralled as a large black and crimson butterfly uncurled itself and seemed to flicker into life. There is also an insect and reptile room with an assortment of tarantulas, ants, bees, iguanas and frogs. A microscope is set up with slides of butterfly wings and eggs and the staff were very helpful, even inviting the children to stroke an iguana.

There is a film room and the shop has a good range of cards, books and games on the natural world theme. You can return to the glasshouse for another look later in the day as long as you have your hand stamped when you go in.

Preston Hall has plenty of other things to see. The Museum includes a Victorian high street with every imaginable shop from hat shop to sweet shop, their windows full of period pieces. There are several craftsmen carrying on their trade there: a cobbler making slippers, a farrier, a toy-maker and a blacksmith in his forge. On some

☞ Sundays a Northumbrian pipe maker demonstrates his skills. Our children particularly enjoyed the printers shop where they watched pictures being printed from old copper blocks. Upstairs there are a large number of period rooms from Victorian times and a collection of children's toys. There is a shop here too selling cards, toys and gifts. Buggies are not allowed in the house and have to be left at the entrance.

Outside there is still more – if you've got the stamina – several play areas, a wildfowl walk, a tropical aviary and crazy golf. The park stretches down to the river where you can walk or fish, while beside the house there are acres of lawn for picnicking and playing.

Fact File

- ADDRESS Butterfly World, Preston Park, Yarm Road, Stockton on Tees, Cleveland
- TELEPHONE 01642 791414 (Butterfly World) or 01642 781184 (Museum)
- DIRECTIONS A19 south from Tyne Tunnel, turn onto A66, then south to Yarm on the A135. Preston Park is 1/4 mile further on
- PUBLIC TRANSPORT Buses from Stockton to Yarm
- DISTANCE 45 miles
- TRAVEL TIME 50 minutes
- OPENING 10.00am-5.30pm (4.00pm in winter) daily
- PRICES £2.75 adults, £2.00 children, under-5's free. Museum free. Car park £1.00
- RESTAURANT FACILITIES In Museum
- NAPPY CHANGING FACILITIES Yes
- HIGH CHAIRS Yes
- DOGS Park only
- PUSHCHAIR-FRIENDLY Yes
- NEARBY Green Dragon Museum, Stockton on Tees (01642 674308), a local heritage museum

The Hancock Museum

. . . every creeping thing that creeps upon the earth

THIS IS AN EXCELLENT PLACE TO WHILE AWAY A DAMP SUNDAY afternoon. Essentially a Natural History museum with a fine collection of bird and insect specimens, inspired curators have created two other fascinating galleries: The Living Planet environmental display, and Land of the Pharoahs, an ancient Egyptian display. Both are full of hands-on activities, puzzles, computer programmes and recordings, bringing history and ecology alive for young and old. Besides these there is a temporary exhibition downstairs which in recent years has included the rainforest, big cats, and the land of the dinosaurs – each a real highlight for children.

If you take the right-hand entrance to the Museum and keep to the right you will find Abel's Ark, always our first port of call. It is a taxidermist's dream; dozens of stuffed animals and birds trooping towards an ark, wombat with spiny anteater, buffalo with lioness, all splendidly lifelike. Just around the corner are the live specimens, snakes, turtles, fish and leaf-cutting ants scurrying across their tank with impossibly large leaves on their back.

> **"Full of hands-on activities, puzzles, computer programmes and recordings"**

Upstairs, go through the doors on the right to follow the galleries in order. The collection of birds is huge and immaculately displayed. Though some of them are 150 years old, their feathers have not faded and there is plenty to interest children: recognising garden and sea birds, marvelling at the small and the large, the exotic and the rare. The only drawback is the height of the cabinets, meaning small children need to be lifted for a proper view.

☞ Next is the insect gallery which boasts fabulous displays of butterflies, moths and beetles, this time with benches below for children to climb on and look.

Don't miss the honey bee observation hive on the landing outside, then take a left for the Ancient Greeks and Land of the Pharoahs. This is an excellent exhibition taking you through displays of farming, home life, death and the gods. Children can have a go at grinding corn, building a pyramid and making an Egyptian tile pattern. The highlight, talked about long after in our household, is the embalmer's tent and the two Hancock mummies. Be warned – the tent is quite scary: inside are life-sized models of the embalmer removing the innards from a corpse. It is wise for anyone squeamish to hurry past. Next are the mummies, one shown unwrapped, shrivelled and shining in a rock-cut tomb, and the other still bandaged inside her painted wooden coffin. There is a fascinating computer programme about the re-building of her face using X-ray and computer simulation. You can inspect the result by looking at the model alongside.

Do leave time for the Living Planet, the hands-on environmental gallery downstairs. This tackles a range of themes, from food chains to endangered species and energy saving. Children can look at slides under a microscope, identify birds and butterflies using a computer data base and design their own animals.

There is a small cafe on the ground floor and a gift shop full of natural history and dinosaur merchandise, plenty at pocket money prices. Near the giant globe is a brass-rubbing area, paper is 3p a sheet and crayons can be borrowed from the shop for children to create their very own cheap souvenir.

Fact File

- ADDRESS The Hancock Museum, Barras Bridge, Newcastle, Tyne & Wear
- TELEPHONE 0191 222 7418
- DIRECTIONS On a low hill opposite the Civic Centre. Car parking outside or in Newcastle Playhouse
- PUBLIC TRANSPORT Haymarket Metro
- DISTANCE in city centre
- TRAVEL TIME 0
- OPENING All year, 10.00am-5.00pm Monday to Saturday, 2.00pm-5.00pm Sunday
- PRICES Adults £1.95, children £1.00, under-4's free
- RESTAURANT FACILITIES Yes
- NAPPY CHANGING FACILITIES No
- HIGH CHAIRS Yes
- DOGS No
- PUSHCHAIR-FRIENDLY Yes
- NEARBY Newcastle city centre with shops and restaurants or Laing art gallery in Higham Place (0191 232 7734)

Killhope Leadmining Centre

DON'T BE PUT OFF BY THE UNINSPIRING NAME; EVEN ON A DRIZZLY DAY there is plenty here for young and old. Kids will love prospecting for lead and collecting pockets full of treasure while parents can ponder on the rigours of the miners' lives and the drudgery of the mining process.

Killhope in upper Weardale is the most complete leadmining site in Britain and the centre has been set out very imaginatively. There is plenty of hands-on activity both inside and out to involve even the smallest child although parents may have to do a bit of explaining along the way.

Beginning at the Visitor Centre youngsters are immediately invited to look for pictures of Mr Sopwith and his telescope (the original mine owner) which are posted high and low throughout the exhibition. Outside, the marked route takes you to an original building called the Mineshop where you can explore the miners' cramped quarters, the agents' office, the smithy and the stable. Older children can dress up and parade around in Victorian-style clothes while younger ones dabble with the agent's ink pen or hammer on the blacksmith's anvil.

"Quartz, fool's gold and amethyst to be found and hammers for splitting stones"

Down the path is the Washing Rake which immediately became the focus of our children's visit. Here boys used to separate lead ore from other unwanted minerals by shovelling, raking, sieving and picking. You can try all these yourselves and keep anything you find! Our three-year-old had a whale of a time wielding a huge spade and pushing muddy stones into the water channel (wellies would be an idea even on a dry day). Meanwhile his older sister perched on the edge of the hotching tubs, (two huge wooden sieves of stones) and ferreted around for booty. There is quartz, fool's gold and amethyst to be found and hammers for splitting stones. The museum staff wander around this area explaining the processes and encouraging everyone to have a go. Listen for the cheer when a lump of gleaming grey lead is discovered!

Nearby is the old mine entrance. You can don a hard hat, hat lamp and overshoes and go down on a guided tour. The tour lasts 45 minutes and is wet, rough and dark, probably not for young children, but an incomparable insight into the working conditions of miners if you can stand it. The mine visit is charged separately.

Out in the air again and on up the hill is the mill with its magnificent working waterwheel. Built by Lord Armstrong it is a wheel of superlatives: 33' 8" in diameter and weighing 18 tons, it carries 72 buckets of water. There is no access for buggies as the buildings are all up steps, but it is worth letting toddlers scramble up themselves as the wheel is awe-inspiring. Behind the mill there is a 30-minute woodland walk which explores the mine water supply system and passes older mining remains, definitely backpack not buggy territory as there are some steep climbs.

On the way out drop into the local minerals exhibition next to the agent's office. There are some splendid specimens and giant magnifying glasses to look through, all at toddler height.

Fact File

- ADDRESS Killhope Lead Mining Centre, Upper Weardale, County Durham
- TELEPHONE 01388 537505
- DIRECTIONS On A689 between Alston and Stanhope, 2 miles west of Cowshill. Follow the brown signs from Alston
- PUBLIC TRANSPORT Express bus from Newcastle to Stanhope; OK Travel bus from Durham. Weardale Motor Services 101 is extended to Killhope by arrangement (01388 528235)
- DISTANCE 50 miles
- TRAVEL TIME 1 hour 30 minutes
- OPENING Daily April to end October, 10.30am-5.00pm. Last admission 4.30pm. Sundays only in November
- PRICES Adults £3.00, children £1.50, under-5's free, family £7.50. Mine £1.60 adults, 80p children
- RESTAURANT FACILITIES Yes
- NAPPY CHANGING FACILITIES Yes
- HIGH CHAIRS Yes
- DOGS Yes
- PUSHCHAIR-FRIENDLY Partly
- NEARBY Weardale Museum at Irehopesburn (01388 537417). Heritage centre at Allenheads. Plenty of walks and picnic spots

National Railway Museum

YES — IT'S A LONG WAY TO TRAVEL FOR A DAY OUT, BUT THIS IS A marvellous place, worth a full day's visit and you can make a treat of it by going there and back on the train, which is quicker than driving. Pace yourselves by interspersing the big trains with spells in the indoor or outdoor playgrounds, and save your visit to the superb interactive Magician's Road until spirits are in need of a revival.

The museum consists of two enormous halls, the South Hall and the Great Hall, with a subway between where you can leave coats in lockers. There is also an outdoor area, South Yard, with miniature railway rides, a play area and Magician's Road. As you go in ask about special events: on our visit we watched a turntable demonstration and an excellent 20-minute play about railway navvies.

In the Great Hall begin at the huge central turntable. This is operated twice a day and can turn the biggest of engines, manoeuvring the locomotives on and off for work or storage. Twenty four gleaming engines stand around it like the rays of the sun, a spectacular sight. Look for the engine which you can walk right underneath, peering up at its great chains and mechanisms, and the engine which has been sliced in half. There are steps alongside many of the carriages on display, allowing you to have a good peer inside. We particularly enjoyed the Royal Mail display, where the children tried a pneumatic pump, felt the weight of mail bags, sorted letters and did a computer quiz.

> **"Twenty four gleaming engines stand around the central turntable like the rays of the sun"**

On the opposite side of the hall you'll find a model railway with engines tootling round a large track layout. There are steps up so that even toddlers get a good view.

☞

Our two-year-old loved it and would have stayed all day watching the trains going in and out of tunnels. Nearby, until April 1997, is the Channel Tunnel exhibition, to be replaced then by an interactive area of railway toys and games. Have a look at Mallard alongside, the gleaming holder of the world speed record for a steam loco (126 mph).

Over in the South Hall there are more trains to admire, some of which you can climb on. There is a large exhibition of Royal carriages, including one used by Queen Victoria. The interiors are suitably plush, and waxwork figures inside help children imagine what it was like for such wealthy passengers.

Outside in South Yard there are steam and diesel locos and working replicas of Stephenson's Rocket and Iron Duke. These are operated at weekends and holidays when you can have a free ride. If none of the big engines is going there is a miniature one to sit astride and chuff up and down a short track. You may need to queue as it only carries a few passengers at a time, but alongside is a children's playground and plenty of benches. Then there is the excellent Magician's Road to visit, an active learning gallery explaining some of the principles behind railway operations. Undoubtedly the biggest hit with our party, do leave yourself enough time for this. There are many practical and ingenious things to try, from building a bridge, working a signal box and wheeltapping, to 'driving' an Intercity train, pushing tubs of coal and laying a miniature track in a battle against the clock.

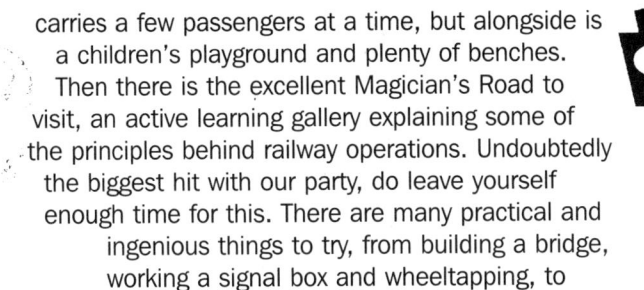

The restaurant in the middle of South Hall has meals and snacks, or you can picnic in the area next to the indoor playground. The museum shop sells all kinds of souvenirs, some at pocket money prices. Take note of the toilet locations: in the Great Hall and next to the shop, but none in the South Hall or South Yard, and it is quite a long walk back from Magician's Road to the central toilets.

Fact File

- ADDRESS National Railway Museum, Leeman Road, York, N. Yorkshire
- TELEPHONE 0800 269658
- DIRECTIONS Tyne Tunnel south and A19 to York. In the city centre follow signs to station and then museum. Car park at north entrance
- PUBLIC TRANSPORT Train to York. 10-minute walk from station
- DISTANCE 80 miles
- TRAVEL TIME 1 hour 30 minutes
- OPENING Daily 10.00am-6.00pm. Last admission one hour earlier
- PRICES Adults £4.50, children £2.50, under-5's free, family £12.00
- RESTAURANT FACILITIES Yes
- NAPPY CHANGING FACILITIES Yes
- HIGH CHAIRS Yes
- DOGS No
- PUSHCHAIR-FRIENDLY Yes
- NEARBY York has other museums and attractions. Try walking on the city walls for a change

Newcastle Discovery Museum

THIS IS THE OLD MUSEUM OF SCIENCE AND ENGINEERING WHICH HAS shot itself into the 90's with exciting new galleries on science, history, the city and fashion. There are flashing lights, games, computers, music and audio tapes to persuade every visitor to participate, and the ingenuity of the hands-on ideas knows no bounds. The original pioneer and maritime galleries are still there for those who like large steam engines and model ships, and there is plenty to fill a rainy day with children of any age. With a soft play area upstairs and some large construction toys downstairs, toddlers are well catered for too. Finally, a most welcome surprise these days, admission is free.

The Museum has a grand entrance to the right of the building and you are immediately in a spectacular new gallery which houses the 100' vessel Turbinia, built on the Tyne and once the world's fastest ship. Don't spend too long here though as there is plenty more to see. Head upstairs to the Science Factory next: a popular destination for school trips so it's worth going early and having a go before the place gets invaded.

> "Children can have a ball trying everything out"

The gallery is devoted to showing that science can be fun. Complex scientific ideas have been interpreted in imaginative and accessible ways – children can have a ball trying everything out while adults or older kids use the copious information boards to relate the fun to the theories. Particularly popular with our children and their friends are the Bernoulli effect ball dancing miraculously on a jet of air; a human kaleidoscope inside which you can hold hands with yourself eight times over (my son played 'ring-a-roses' all on his own); and the Chromakey. This is a special effects booth which allows you to see yourselves on television apparently flying through the air Superman-style above the River Tyne. As a consequence of the technical process, blue clothes become invisible so it is possible to appear as disembodied arms, feet and head, which looks even more wild!

The darkrooms hold a laser show, coloured lights to blend, a see-through mirror and a plasma globe. The latter is a real science fiction item, with glowing light inside which sparks towards your palms as you lay them on the glass. My own favourite is the Hydraulics Conveyor: a Heath Robinson-type contraption with conveyor belts, trolleys, and a pair of giant claws. By following the instructions meticulously (or else it doesn't work), you operate a series of buttons and levers to send a large cube on its course around the machine. Very satisfying!

Next to the Science Factory is the Time Tunnel, a winding gallery which gives you a flying tour of Newcastle's history from the Romans to the present day. It is best for those who can read themselves and contains various trails to follow. For younger children there are a few items which catch the eye and sound effects to listen to, such as the stone effigy of a knight and the model of the old Tyne bridge with shops and houses built across in the Medieval section.

The Pioneer's Gallery and the Maritime Gallery are also on this floor. These are traditional-style galleries, with static exhibits dedicated to Tyneside inventors and inventions and ships. There are some large steam engines and plenty of models to look at. The exhibits are above toddler height so you will need to lift little ones up for a good view.

Don't miss the Great City, an exhibition which celebrates Newcastle's history from 1914 to the present day. It is well put-together with a mixture of tableaux, photographs, and audio-visual effects, as well as displays of the everyday flotsam and jetsam of each decade. There are plenty of hands-on activities to keep little people interested, beginning with a large painting of Newcastle citizens with holes to poke their heads through and mirrors behind so children can see themselves dressed in 1920s attire. Throughout the exhibition there are matchbox museums, sets of little drawers to open with bits and pieces to look at inside, 'feely' boxes and other games for children to play, such as a giant mix and match costume puzzle and a large magnetic jigsaw.

At the end of the Great City is the People's Gallery which showcases aspects of life in modern Newcastle, as seen by people living in the city. Exhibitions here are temporary but there is a permanent corner set up as an indoor play area with a Wendy house and giant construction toys, which offer children a welcome breather after all that looking!

Fact File

- ADDRESS Newcastle Discovery Museum, Blandford Square, Newcastle, Tyne & Wear
- TELEPHONE 0191 232 6789
- DIRECTIONS Car parking meters in Blandford Square. Museum is signposted from Westgate Road and Westmorland Road
- PUBLIC TRANSPORT 10-minute walk from the Central Station and the Metro
- DISTANCE in city centre
- TRAVEL TIME 0
- OPENING 10.00am-5.00pm Monday to Saturday, Sunday 2.00pm-5.00pm
- PRICES Free
- RESTAURANT FACILITIES Yes
- NAPPY CHANGING FACILITIES Yes
- HIGH CHAIRS Yes
- DOGS No
- PUSHCHAIR-FRIENDLY Yes
- NEARBY Eldon Square shopping centre. Laing Art Gallery in Higham Place has Children's gallery and interactive displays (0191 232 7734)

Tynemouth Sealife Centre

I'd like to be under the sea, in an octopus's garden . . .

ON THE GRAND PARADE ABOVE TYNEMOUTH LONG SANDS, THE SEA Life Centre is a first rate aquarium. Here you come literally eyeball to eyeball with sea creatures as they swim about in tanks above, below and all around. Everyone is encouraged to touch and feel the creatures, and even the smallest can watch a ray or a shark nosing up against the glass only inches away from his or her pushchair. Your hand is stamped as you enter so you can go in and out as you wish throughout the day. Have a first look, then maybe a stint down on the beach or round the boating lake just across the road, and then come back to watch a feeding demonstration.

The first tanks you come to are freshwater ones with fish from the Tyne Estuary. These are not sterile tanks sealed off on all sides but large open pools with rocks, seaweed and a wave machine which keeps the water swirling to and fro. Large fish swim up and down while eels dart amongst them. Murals of the seashore and clever lighting combine to create an exciting atmosphere and children are thrilled by the immediacy of it all. The tanks in the next section show creatures found on the harbour wall and in the offshore waters. There is a stunning collection of sea anemones, with tentacles gently waving, a large conger eel, and an interesting display of starfish. Our children's favourite was the octopus, crouching over her eggs inside a large jar, while their

> "Our children's favourite was the octopus, crouching over her eggs inside a large jar"

HEINZ GUIDE TO DAYS OUT WITH KIDS **45**

friends were particularly taken with the wrecked boat hull and rusty anchor which the fish were swimming amongst. The route through this part of the centre is somewhat narrow and winding, causing a buggy bottleneck on a busy day. The tanks are also too high for toddlers who need to be lifted up. However it's the only awkward area, elsewhere there are steps for small people to stand on.

The next section is Close Encounters where there is a large pool full of rays. You can look at them from a small platform above or lean over the rail and touch them. They are used to being handfed and swim readily towards your fingers, rising to nose at them and allowing you to stroke their graceful bodies. Our five-year-old loved touching the rays, but she did need to be lifted up. If you are there at feeding time you may be able to offer them a snack and feel the strange ticklish sensation of their mouths.

Next you come to the Jelly Lab showing the entire life-cycle of jellyfish and other stinging fish. They are kept in subtly-lit tanks which make them look far more beautiful then they ever do when you meet them in the sea yourself. In the Sea Lab and Fish Nursery next door you can see baby sharks and rays at various stages of development and there is a rock pool with crabs, anemones and starfish which may be gently handled. There are talks on the hour and zoom-in TV on the rock pools.

The final part of the centre is the highlight – an ocean tunnel where sharks, eels and other fish glide above and beside you as you walk through. It is an amazing sensation coming face-to-face with these creatures in their strange and silent world.

If your children need a break from all this looking and touching at any point there is an outdoor adventure playground next to the Sea Lab or a small soft play area upstairs. Sammy's Restaurant offers a good variety of snacks, hot and cold meals. Take a look at the blackboard by the entrance as it gives times of any demonstrations, film shows and feeding times.

Fact File

- ADDRESS Tynemouth Sea Life Centre, Grand Parade, Beaconsfield, Tynemouth, Tyne & Wear
- TELEPHONE 0191 257 6100
- DIRECTIONS A1058 from Newcastle, follow signs to seafront. Sea Life is on the coast road, midway between Tynemouth and Cullercoats
- PUBLIC TRANSPORT 10 minutes walk from Cullercoats metro
- DISTANCE 7 miles
- TRAVEL TIME 15 minutes
- OPENING Daily 10.00am-7.00pm (4.00pm winter)
- PRICES Adults £4.50, children £3.25, under-4's free
- RESTAURANT FACILITIES Yes
- NAPPY CHANGING FACILITIES Yes
- HIGH CHAIRS Yes
- DOGS No
- PUSHCHAIR-FRIENDLY Yes
- NEARBY The picturesque ruins of Tynemouth Castle & Priory (0191 257 1090), or the rock pools and birdwatching around St Mary's Lighthouse (0191 252 0853)

Washington Wildfowl & Wetland Centre

*Doing the goose step –
Pit pat paddle pat!*

IF YOU LIKE BIRDS THIS IS A GREAT PLACE TO SPEND THE DAY. THERE are 100 acres of lake, woodland and wetland with as many different species of birds. Forget all those afternoons handing out crusts to overfed ducks at the local pond, here the ducks and geese clamour to be fed and will even eat from your hand. The tamer ones will waddle amongst the children delighting toddlers as they nose at their pockets for food. Further away in the water are the larger birds, majestically balanced on one leg or stretching their massive wings: flamingos, Trumpeter swans, black swans, herons, King Eiders, Emperor geese. You can walk, picnic, watch from bird hides or from the restaurant terrace and with a large play area too, there is plenty to keep everyone busy. In winter many more birds visit and you may see some unusual species. Ask at the entrance what to look out for. However, if you do visit in winter, the paths are quite exposed, so take lots of warm clothes, also it can be very muddy if the weather has been wet, so bring wellies.

> "As well as the common birds there are plenty more exotic species"

Buy the walkabout guide to the park for £1.00 before you begin as it is a large place and difficult to judge distances once you have set off. From the visitor building there is a circular route which will take about an hour, more than that with stops to feed and look. It is quite a hike for little legs so take a buggy and carry some food supplies, as all the amenities are at the beginning of the walk.

Bags of food are on sale for 30p at the entrance. Children can get right down to the water's edge and have a good look. Geese, ducks and swans wander freely and are generally very friendly. There are some shallow steps further round where kids can sit and feed the ducks by hand. Although small children and water are generally a lethal combination, if you keep a close eye on the kids at these points the rest is fairly safe. Encourage the kids to save a bit of their food for the birds on the far side. Usually the bags have long since been emptied and the birds over there seem particularly grateful for any small offerings!

The path moves away from the lake's edge and continues in a wide circle with pens on either side. Most of the birds are fairly visible though you may have to lift toddlers sometimes for a view of the shyer ones. As well as the more common birds there are plenty more exotic species. Our children adore the pink flamingos, with their curving beaks and knobbly knees. The black swans are also favourites. In the afternoon join the warden on his feeding round at 3.00pm, as he gives a good commentary. It's also a chance to see the birds at closer range as they all rush to the fence when they see him coming with his barrow.

For a longer walk in a wilder area take the path on the right opposite the conservatory. It is rougher terrain with some shallow steps but it is still possible to take a buggy down here and you can walk for another hour through woodland, beside a number of other ponds. There are viewing points and hides and although the birds are further away you are watching them in more natural surroundings. If you're lucky you will catch glimpses of the herons on the heron pond, and at the edge of the frog pond watch out for the tadpoles in springtime.

Back on the main circuit there is a boardwalk over a wetland area which children enjoy. In summer you will see plenty of insect life, such as dragonflies and damselflies, as well as the birds. You will also find plenty to look at in the nursery which is open from May to August. Here eggs are incubated in outdoor and indoor pens, and young birds reared. Since the babies tend to be huddled on the furthest banks of the ponds, the nursery offers a great chance to see them in all their fluffy newness. Nearby is an excellent play area and, in warm weather, an ice-cream kiosk.

Back at the visitor building there is a restaurant and shop, and an excellent Wetland Discovery Centre, explaining wetland systems through interactive computer games, a video, a giant jigsaw and other hands-on displays. It has a number of large boxes with beaks, wings, skeletons, feet and eggs inside for children to handle. Many are set up as clues in puzzles which children can solve using the specimens as evidence.

Fact File

- ADDRESS Wildfowl and Wetland Centre, District 15, Washington, Tyne & Wear
- TELEPHONE 0191 416 5454
- DIRECTIONS Through the Tyne tunnel and south on the A19. Well-signposted from there
- PUBLIC TRANSPORT X4 bus from Newcastle, Mondays-Saturdays
- DISTANCE 15 miles
- TRAVEL TIME 25 minutes
- OPENING Daily 9.30am-5.30pm (summer), one hour before dusk in winter
- PRICES Adults £4.00, children £2.40, under-4's free
- RESTAURANT FACILITIES Yes
- NAPPY CHANGING FACILITIES Yes
- HIGH CHAIRS Yes
- DOGS No
- PUSHCHAIR-FRIENDLY Yes
- NEARBY Washington Old Hall (0191 416 6879), and Penshaw monument

Woodhorn Colliery Museum

Gannin' doon the pit

THERE AREN'T MANY PLACES WHERE YOU CAN CLIMB ON A COLLIERY winding wheel or peer up a mineshaft towards the daylight as if you are down the pit yourself. For the miners who once worked down Woodhorn Colliery and still live in the villages round about, it must be a bitter-sweet experience to see their old place of work turned into a museum. For visitors though, it is a marvellous opportunity to learn something about the industry upon which much of the local area depended for 200 years. For children, there is the thrill of seeing the original winding wheel in action and watching a working blacksmith, a furniture-maker and a guitar-maker. There is also a train ride in the grounds of the museum. A diesel locomotive which once pulled coal trucks down in the pit has been restored and pulls several open carriages the half mile or so down to the lake in The Queen Elizabeth II Country Park and back. The train runs most days unless there is bad weather or a maintenance problem. There is a small charge (70p adults, 40p children), but this will be the only ticket you buy all day as the rest of the museum is free.

> "You can watch a furniture maker, a blacksmith and a guitar-maker at work"

The museum is housed in the original pit buildings with a large green field in the middle. There is a play area on the green with swings and climbing equipment suitable for under-7's, so the kids can take a breather.

Beginning in the main building, the displays trace the history of mining through the 18th and 19th centuries. You can ponder on the harshness of life then and point out the pictures of child trappers and pit ponies to your own children. There is a lot of explaining to do but the lifesized models and artefacts help to grab their attention. The photographs and sound effects help too. My son was intrigued by the underground train and the wounded figure on a stretcher.

Upstairs the displays give an idea of how families used to live in the 1930's. There is a miner sitting in his social club and a housewife in her kitchen. Some children may find the continuous dialogue of the soundtrack a bit frightening and have trouble relating it to the models, but there's no such trouble with the pigeon loft and the row of prize-winning leeks: Geordie legends if ever there were!

Back on the ground floor there is an art gallery with some evocative work by local artists, members of the Ashington Group. There's also a colliery locomotive on show as part of a history of colliery railways.

You will find the resident craftspeople in various buildings around the green. If you strike lucky you can watch a furniture maker, a blacksmith and a guitar-maker at work. Also alongside is the Engine Turning Room, definitely worth a visit though there are two steep flights of steps to climb. This houses the huge wheel that used to draw in and pay out the cable attached to the cages transporting the men up and down the mine. A member of the museum staff is eager to demonstrate the mechanism and willingly answers questions as the bells ring and the wheel slowly turns.

There is one other outbuilding with an exhibition about the Northumberland miners' union. It has fascinating pictures and documents, probably of little interest for children though they may like to see the six miners' banners on display.

There is a cafe serving good home-made fare. You can have a three-course dinner or soup and sandwiches, the service is relaxed and friendly and the cakes delicious too. No one minded the debris left behind after our assorted crew had left the table.

The museum is in the Queen Elizabeth II Country Park, which has a lake, woodland and an hotel. You can walk down to the lake or drive round to the hotel car park just along the road and set out from there.

Fact File

- ADDRESS Woodhorn Colliery Museum, Queen Elizabeth II Country Park, Ashington, Northumberland
- TELEPHONE 01670 856968
- DIRECTIONS Take the Great North Road (A6125) turning onto the A189 and continuing north past Ashington turnoff. Follow signs to Queen Elizabeth II Park
- PUBLIC TRANSPORT Buses X31, X33 and 437 from Newcastle to Woodhorn
- DISTANCE 20 miles
- TRAVEL TIME 30 minutes
- OPENING Wednesday-Sunday, 11.00am-5.00pm (May to October), and 10.00am-4.00pm (November to April)
- PRICES Free
- RESTAURANT FACILITIES Yes
- NAPPY CHANGING FACILITIES No
- HIGH CHAIRS Yes
- DOGS Outside only
- PUSHCHAIR-FRIENDLY Yes
- NEARBY The beautiful Druridge Bay for dunes, lake, trees and birdwatching

The Great Outdoors

Bellingham

REMEMBER THOSE DAYS BEFORE CHILDREN WHEN YOU'D PUT ON YOUR walking boots and actually cover some miles? Well, Bellingham is a place with a couple of walks near town which are short enough for little legs yet still pass through some delightful countryside.

Bellingham (pronounced "Bellinjam") is a small stone-built town on the banks of the North Tyne river. In the heart of Northumberland, it is bordered by some wonderful country, with Kielder Forest to the west, and the North Tyne valley. You can enjoy views of the heather-clad moors as you drive up. Watch out for the cyclists, the town is a popular lunch stop with mountain bikers and has several cafes serving hearty fare.

> "Sit by the burn for a while and let the kids splash around"

The first child-friendly walk is a two-mile stroll along the banks of the river. Park in the middle of the town and walk down through Manchester Square. Take the narrow lane on the left of the square and walk down to the bridge over Hareshaw Burn, a stream running down to the river. Once across the bridge you need to turn right and follow the path over a stile and through a private garden down to the river. The path is narrow and can be overgrown in summer but it is quiet and green and very pleasant. You can turn back when you reach a gate leading on to a farm road. A track on the left here leads back to where you started. If everyone is game, go on for another mile up the farm road, past the farm and continue along beside the river until the path crosses a narrow stream. Walk up across the field on the left until you reach a road. This leads back to the town.

The second walk is perhaps more of an outing although still only three miles there and back. Its destination is Hareshaw Linn, a dramatic 30' waterfall with a small cave cut into the rock below, where you can stand and watch. It is lovely in autumn as the path leads through a valley of mixed woodland. Last time, the kids came home with handfuls of leaves – gold, russet, crimson and orange – all carefully gathered from the path.

You can park in town and walk to the start, or there is a small car park just by the footpath. From the main square, take the road signposted for Redesmouth. There is a bridge over Hareshaw Burn almost immediately and the road to the car park is next left. The path is signed and the way is clear. You pass a farm at the beginning and then walk through an area of grassy hillocks. These are the remains of coal and iron-mining works and make excellent hills for rolling down or playing 'king of the castle'. The path carries on up to a stile at the entrance to the woods, but if you sit by the burn for a while, the kids can splash around and it's a lovely spot for a picnic.

The first stretch of woodland is quite steep; don't despair though, keep the kids going up to the seat at the top, and then the rest of the walk will be easy. From there the path re-descends to the burn and winds back and forth across no less than seven footbridges before finally reaching the rocky canyon and the waterfall at the head of the valley. There is endless scope for hiding and ambushing, pooh sticks or (our family favourite) playing the three billy goats gruff. The views downstream and through the trees are quite beautiful, particularly on a sunny day when shafts of light catch the water and dapple the path.

Don't plan on stopping long at the waterfall since the cave is actually quite chilly. It is damp with spray and always in shade, so save your snacks until you're back down the valley again. Better still, eat on the hop with the promise of tea in one of Bellingham's cafes when you get back. There is a good selection of pubs and tearooms in the town, all on the main street, so take your pick when you return. If you are interested in old buildings take a look at the 13th century St Cuthbert's church, a solid stone church with a fine stone roof and slit windows, built originally to withstand attacks from marauding Scots.

Fact File

- ADDRESS Bellingham, Hexham, Northumberland
- TELEPHONE Tourist Information 01434 220616
- DIRECTIONS A69 to Hexham, A6079 to Chollerford and B6320 to Bellingham
- PUBLIC TRANSPORT Bus from Newcastle on summer Sundays
- DISTANCE 30 miles
- TRAVEL TIME 1 hour
- OPENING Anytime
- PRICES Free
- RESTAURANT FACILITIES Yes
- NAPPY CHANGING FACILITIES No
- HIGH CHAIRS In some restaurants
- DOGS Yes
- PUSHCHAIR-FRIENDLY No
- NEARBY Kielder Lake and Forest for miles of footpaths, play areas and picnic sites, with watersports, cycling and pony trekking too

Belsay Hall

When you wake up to a fine morning and everyone is ready for a full day out, go to Belsay. Not far from Newcastle, it has plenty to amuse the children. Besides the Hall, there is a castle to explore and 30 acres of landscaped parkland and gardens, ranging from formal beds and lawns with clipped hedges to mature woodland, rhododendrons and azaleas. The highlight for our family is the quarry garden, set dramatically within rocky cliffs and dripping with green vegetation. Here, where the plants grow impossibly large leaves and the rocks are green and slimy, there is an almost prehistoric feel to the place as if it has been created as the backdrop for a dinosaur film. Hide and seek, or ambush games take on a whole new dimension!

Begin your visit in the neo-Grecian Hall, although entirely unfurnished, large empty rooms hold more attraction for kids than you might expect and ours love running from one room to another hearing their footsteps echo. A visit to the vast wine cellars is a must, again empty but invitingly spooky, full of dark shadows and cold stone. (Take care on the rather crumbly steps down.) The old bottle compartments are marked with letters of the alphabet and our five-year-old insisted on spelling out her name before we returned to the fresh air.

> **"A quarry garden set dramatically within rocky cliffs and dripping with green vegetation"**

Outside the Hall are formal gardens, terraces planted with shrubs and flowers and a rose garden. For plant lovers there are some unusual shrubs and everything is blooming and burgeoning. Along the path there is a croquet lawn still used for matches, you may be lucky enough to hit upon a game and can sit and watch the players in their whites swinging mallets at the balls, or retiring to rest in the wooden summer house, just like a scene from Brideshead Revisited.

Going through the door in the wall beside the croquet lawn you arrive in the woods and there's a pleasant walk through the rhododendrons to the quarry garden. All the paths are passable with a pushchair. Emerging from the shadows of the quarry, there are open fields ahead. Down to the left is the castle, the original home of the Middleton family, owners of Belsay for 600 years. Although now in ruins, one castle tower can still be climbed and there are fabulous views from the top. It is safe to take children up as the top is well-fenced on all sides. Back at ground level there are rooms to explore, a dark hidey hole to run in, and a pleasant grassy area to sit. If you have brought a picnic this is a good place to eat it. There are also picnic benches under the trees in the car park.

Back at the Hall there is a cafe serving light lunches and teas. There is an exhibition about Belsay upstairs above the shop. The shop sells the usual cards, books and gifts and there is often a plant stall outside too. Toilets are beside the car park, right back near the entrance, although you can double back to them from the croquet lawn before you go into the woods.

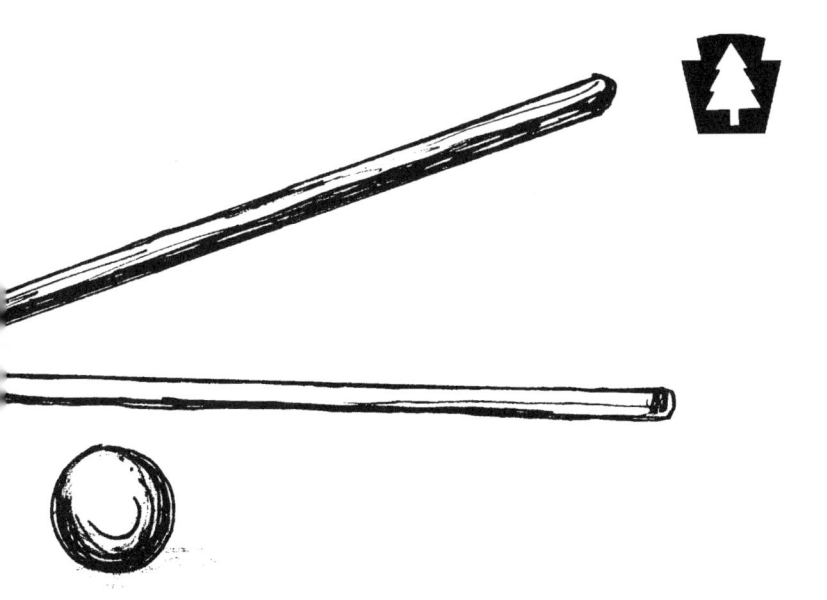

Special events are held throughout the year; concerts, craft fairs, garden tours, a teddy bears' picnic, a falconry display. Telephone for details.

Fact File

- ADDRESS Belsay Hall, Belsay, Northumberland
- TELEPHONE 01661 881636
- DIRECTIONS A696 from Newcastle to Belsay
- PUBLIC TRANSPORT Buses from Newcastle and Morpeth (Vasey's/Snaith's 808 or Northumbria 506/8)
- DISTANCE 14 miles
- TRAVEL TIME 25 minutes
- OPENING Daily 10.00am-6.00pm (4.00pm in winter)
- PRICES Adults £3.50, children £1.80, under-5's and English Heritage members free
- RESTAURANT FACILITIES Yes
- NAPPY CHANGING FACILITIES Yes
- HIGH CHAIRS Yes
- DOGS Yes
- PUSHCHAIR-FRIENDLY Yes
- NEARBY Aydon Castle, a 13th century manor house in Corbridge (01434 632450)

Cragside Country Park

*Build it up with iron and steel,
my fair lady*

GO TO CRAGSIDE WHEN EVERYONE IS IN THE MOOD FOR A GOOD WALK. The mansion is set in a thousand acres of woodland, with lakes and streams and forty miles of footpaths. You may not cover much of that with kids in tow but it is a lovely place to stroll and there's more than enough for a full day out. In May you'll catch the rhododendrons in bloom, in summer enjoy the lush greenness of the woods, and in autumn the trees turn gold and red and the paths are thick with dead leaves.

Built for the first Lord Armstrong, Cragside House and grounds are full of examples of his engineering genius. Begin by walking the Power Circuit, a circular walk just over a mile long, starting opposite the Visitor Centre. Too tricky for buggies (take a backpack), the walk takes you from Tumbleton Lake through the woods and up round to the house. Ending with a fairly stiff uphill hike, do it while the kids are fresh. There is plenty to occupy them as you walk, not least counting

> "Six bridges to cross and under the seventh, the Iron Bridge, the first steel bridge in the world"

the bridges you cross. Six in all, and you walk under the seventh, the Iron Bridge, reputed to be the first steel bridge in the world.

The Pump House houses an engine which previously pumped spring water up to a reservoir supplying the house. The kids can press buttons to set the hydraulics in motion while you ponder the fact that when Lord Armstrong had the luxury of running water most people in Newcastle did not have an indoor toilet!

Branch off the Power Walk on the right hand path by the Iron Bridge to see the Formal Garden. There are formal terraces, a grotto with tropical ferns, a conservatory and a goldfish pond (no warning so beware of toddlers running on ahead of you). There are also fabulous views over the Cheviots on a clear day. Back at the bridge walk through the Pinetum, planted with trees brought from all over the world. If you want to curtail the Power Circuit, cut through the Pinetum and go straight up through the rockery to the house. If you've got the energy though, go on through the Debdon Gorge. Here is a waterfall which Armstrong used to make hydro-electricity to serve the house. The original turbine has been restored and can be seen in action at the Power House.

The final part of the circuit is a long haul up to the house. Inside are over 30 rooms on show, too many for young children probably, especially as neither buggies nor backpacks are allowed. If you do go in, there is a wealth of Victorian painting and furniture to see as well as Lord Armstrong's technological innovations.

The Visitor Centre is beyond the car park. It is aimed at older children and adults but worth a quick look round. The Armstrong Energy Centre explores the production of energy from conventional fuels and alternative sources. There are models, pictures and a number of buttons to press.

The Vickers Rooms Restaurant is just next door in the old stables. It sells sandwiches, soup, cakes and drinks. The National Trust shop sells the usual range of goodies with a good selection of books.

There is plenty more to explore in the Country Park, but you'll need to move your car to the various car parks as everything is very spread out. Near Cragend car park you will find the quarry. Blackburn car park is near Blackburn Lake where there is a thatched boathouse and you can picnic beside the water. At Crozier there are fabulous viewpoints and some toilets. Other toilets are at the Visitor Centre and the house. There is a play area beside Dunkirk car park, just by the exit onto the B6344 to Newcastle. It is built in the woodland and has some great climbing equipment, slides and swings. There is not much for very little ones though and it can be muddy.

Fact File

- ADDRESS Cragside House, Rothbury, Morpeth, Northumberland
- TELEPHONE 01669 620333
- DIRECTIONS A1 north, then A697 to Wooler. Take the B6344 to Rothbury. Cragside is a mile north of Rothbury off the B6341
- PUBLIC TRANSPORT Buses 514 and 516 from Newcastle stop at Estate Gate. There is a long walk up to the house
- DISTANCE 30 miles
- TRAVEL TIME 50 minutes
- OPENING Grounds 10.30am-7.00pm daily, except Mondays, 28 March to 31 October. Last admission 5.00pm. Tuesday and weekends only in November and December, closing at dusk
- PRICES Grounds only £3.80 adults, £1.90 children, under-5's free. Under-12's free in school holidays. House extra
- RESTAURANT FACILITIES Yes
- NAPPY CHANGING FACILITIES Yes
- HIGH CHAIRS Yes, no straps
- DOGS Yes, grounds only
- PUSHCHAIR-FRIENDLY Limited
- NEARBY Brinkburn Priory (01665 570628) is a lovely riverside picnic spot

The Farne Islands

A SUMMER BOAT TRIP TO THE FARNE ISLANDS MAKES A WONDERFUL day out. There's the pitch and toss of the boat, the first exciting glimpse of a puffin skimming across the water or the bobbing head of a seal, and then the chance to explore an island and discover nests with eggs and chicks just a foot or so away. Eighteen different species of seabird nest on the islands in the summer and you can see some of them at very close range.

This is definitely a trip to be taken on a fine day and when you're feeling capable. Toddlers need to be closely supervised and little ones really have to be carried in a backpack or sling. However, it offers a unique experience and for our family rates as one of our most exciting days out.

You catch the boat from Seahouses and should telephone for times as these vary according to tides and weather conditions. There's a car park just up from the quayside and toilets on the other side of the road (there are none on the boat and only on Inner Farne island). A number of different companies operate but prices and trips are identical. There is a one and a half hour trip around the islands, but the longer two and half hour trip gives you an hour on an island as well as the boat tour and commentary.

> "The seals swam up quite close and peered at us before diving under and bobbing up again"

Staple Island has the remains of an old lighthouse once manned by the grandfather of Grace Darling. Grace lived in the lighthouse on Longstone Island and it was from there that she and her father carried out their famous rescue.

On Inner Farne there's a small chapel dedicated to St Cuthbert who lived there as a hermit in the 7th century, and a small National Trust Information Centre with displays about the birds and seals.

☞   Before docking on either Inner Farne or Staple Island the boat takes you close to some of the smaller islands where the sight of hundreds of puffins lining the cliffs and whole clouds of terns wheeling above is quite spectacular. Our children were excited by the cormorants and shags diving in and out of the water then perching on the rocks and "hanging out their wings" to dry. Their favourite part though was the seals who swam up quite close and peered at us before diving under and bobbing up again somewhere else.

Once on an island you must keep to the paths, but this does not inhibit your view since the birds are unafraid of visitors and perch and nest everywhere. We were entranced by the sight of two fluffy chicks tussling for food, mouths gaping as the parent tern returned from a fishing trip. Later we peered over the cliff at baby kittiwakes in nests glued to the narrowest of ledges and crannies. Next to them a pair of cormorants clumsily changed shift on top of their nest. Do beware – the terns dive-bomb visitors as they walk along the board walks! It doesn't hurt and our children loved it but keep an eye out, make sure everyone has a hat or a hood and watch out for the baby in the backpack!

You need to bring all your food supplies with you and may have to eat on the hoof as there are limited benches on the islands. Better to snack on the boat and then have fish and chips back at Seahouses where there are various sit down or carry out places (Lewis's near the mini roundabout has highchairs). You can picnic in the garden beside the crazy golf or walk out of town and onto the beach. One final point – whatever the weather be well prepared for the trip with warm and wet weather gear, it is always breezy on the water and the temperature can drop very quickly, we ended up in gloves and scarves on a warm July day when we had set out in shorts.

If you have the energy when you return to Seahouses visit the Marine Life and Fishing Heritage Centre just up from the quayside. This houses a grand collection of seaside flotsam and jetsam and is a great place to potter in for an hour or two. It is on four different levels (with no lift). On the ground level are local fish in tanks, including octopus, crabs and eels. The first floor has an old fishing boat and a touch pool where brave children can dodge the pincers and pick up different kinds of crabs. Reconstructed rooms from a fisherman's cottage and a Farne Island Scene with stuffed animals and birds occupy the second floor. Finally, the top floor has a cooper's workshop and a herring smokehouse (complete with real kippers).

Fact File

- ADDRESS Farne Islands, Seahouses, Northumberland. Information from The National Trust Information Centre, 16 Main Street, Seahouses, Northumberland
- TELEPHONE 01665 721099
- DIRECTIONS A1 to Alnwick, then B1340 to Seahouses
- PUBLIC TRANSPORT Bus from Berwick (01289 330733)
- DISTANCE 50 miles
- TRAVEL TIME 1 hour 15 minutes
- OPENING 1 April to 30 April and 1 August to 30 September both islands open from 10.30am-6.00pm daily. 1 May to 31 July (breeding season) Staple Island 10.30am-1.30pm, Inner Farne 1.30pm-5.00pm daily. Boats leave from the quayside from 10.00am
- PRICES Boat – Adult £5.00, child £4.00, under-4's free. Landing fee per island in breeding season adult £3.80, child £1.90, under-5's free. Rest of season adults £2.90, child £1.45, under-5's free. National Trust members free
- RESTAURANT FACILITIES In Seahouses
- NAPPY CHANGING FACILITIES No
- HIGH CHAIRS In Seahouses
- DOGS No
- PUSHCHAIR-FRIENDLY No
- NEARBY Howick Hall Gardens at Alnwick (01665 577285)

Hardwick Hall

IF YOUR CHILDREN ENJOY POND DIPPING AND POTTERING AROUND amongst ducks then try Hardwick Hall. It is a country park with a long thin lake, footpaths that wind around and across it and a boardwalk nature trail. Based on the 18th century landscaped gardens of Hardwick Hall Manor House, (which is now a hotel) the park boasts several follies as well as a wetland area, once the bed of an ornamental lake.

Be prepared – don't come without fishing nets and buckets! They are the essential accessory here and cannot be purchased on site. There are several landing stages at the water's edge, ideal for dipping and scooping, with sinks just behind to deposit the catch in while you identify it from the thoughtfully-provided picture board. There are minnows, sticklebacks and tadpoles in the water, though our kids caught nothing but duckweed, sticks and a couple of snail shells all day. Strange to say this did not seem to detract from their enjoyment at all, there was much discussion of what

"Several landing stages at the water's edge, ideal for dipping and scooping"

might be caught and by whom and as long as each was wielding a net a happy time was had by all.

There are three car parks, each very near to the lake. If you park in the last one and take the path to the left of the gateway ruin you emerge roughly in the middle of the park. With nets in hand pond dipping will probably be the first activity. If so, follow the path right or left and cross over the water as soon as you can, there are pond dipping areas in both spots, with picnic benches on the right side. When the children have had enough of fishing have a walk around the lake. Between the two pond dip areas there is a child-sized hill fort which was very popular with our crew becoming variously a soldiers' barracks, an enchanted castle and a hospital.

The best way to tackle the rest of the park may be to cross back over to the car park side and then take the path left. On this route you will pass a bird hide where you can watch the mallards, moorhens and coots and might be lucky enough to glimpse a heron. Down by the water's edge there is a water plant display built out over the lake which names the various plants and gives you a bit of information too. Set back behind here is an open field for racing around and playing games, there's also another hide for watching woodland birds.

Back on the lakeside path look out for the beginning of the boardwalk nature trail. This is a one-way walk, there are passing places but they are well spaced and a meeting of two double buggies would cause a serious traffic jam. The walk is great, it takes you through a marshy jungle winding this way and that with cartoon information boards telling you all about the vegetation. Finally back at the car park there is an adventure playground which revives flagging spirits and gives everyone a burst of energy before the journey home.

Fact File

- ADDRESS Hardwick Hall, Sedgefield, County Durham
- TELEPHONE 0191 383 3594
- DIRECTIONS A1(M) south and A689 to Sedgefield. Off the west side of A177 Sedgefield bypass
- PUBLIC TRANSPORT Bus from Durham to Sedgefield Green, then 15-minute walk along marked path
- DISTANCE 30 miles
- TRAVEL TIME 35 minutes
- OPENING All times
- PRICES Free
- RESTAURANT FACILITIES No
- NAPPY CHANGING FACILITIES No
- HIGH CHAIRS No
- DOGS Yes
- PUSHCHAIR-FRIENDLY Yes
- NEARBY Whitworth Hall near Spennymoor (01388 720849) for woodland walks, deer, waterwheel and clock museum

The Leas & Marsden Rock

Let's go fly a kite . . .

ON A GREY AND BLUSTERY DAY, WHEN THE KIDS ARE FED UP WITH THEIR toys and each other and you know you've got to get out, head for The Leas and Marsden Rock in South Shields. Pull on the bobble hats and gloves and let them tear around on the grass flying a kite or chasing a ball. Bring buckets and spades too so you can climb down to the beach for a dig.

The Leas is a broad grassy cliff top area stretching for 300 acres down the coast. The grass is regularly mown and level so it's fine for a run around and the sea breeze will certainly chase away the cobwebs. There's a car park right beside the grass and toilets at the south end (open between April and the end of September). Marsden Bay below The Leas is a splendid stretch of coast with clear waters, rock pools and golden sands. The limestone cliffs and Marsden Rock are also home to the most important seabird colony on the North East coastline.

> "A splendid stretch of coast with clear waters, rock pools and golden sands"

It's a long climb down steep stone steps to the beach but there's an easier way to do it – go into the Marsden Grotto pub and take the lift down. It costs 10p but with all your beach paraphernalia to carry it's worth it and besides the pub down at sea level is a great place to visit. It is hewn out of the cliff and has one room which is actually a cave. It was originally built as a house in the 1780s by a local known as Jack the Blaster and was converted into a pub in the 1820s. It has an indoor children's play area with toys, books and games and serves snacks and a full and children's menu (no highchairs though).

HEINZ GUIDE TO DAYS OUT WITH KIDS **69**

Outside there's plenty to explore. The limestone rock has been weathered and worn to form arches, platforms, pillars and caves, providing the ultimate in adventure playgrounds. On our last visit our older two had a wonderful game of dragons and monsters running in and out of the holes, while the baby sat happily digging and eating sand. In the summer the rocks are home to thousands of nesting birds: kittiwakes, herring gulls, fulmars and cormorants. The kittiwakes nest on the ledges of the rocks and you can see them quite clearly with their young from the beach. The cormorants nest on top of Marsden Rock and are best seen from the cliff top. Bring binoculars if you are interested, you can find out more from an RSPB kiosk on the cliff top.

Postcards and paintings of Marsden Rock itself portray it as a huge arch, as it was until February 1996. Then, one night during a particularly ferocious storm, the top of the arch collapsed leaving two separate stacks. The birds seemed unaffected and nested as usual during the summer. However, there has been some discussion about the stability of the rock and some talk about demolishing it altogether. Nothing has happened yet, but even without the arch it is still a marvellous beach.

On a sunny day with the sand between your toes and everyone busy pottering, the beach will be enough but if it's too chilly to sit around for long, drive a few hundred yards further down the coast and visit Souter Lighthouse. Souter opened in 1871 and remained in operation until 1988, now it's a museum complete with fog horns, the Lighthouse Keeper's cottage and an engine room with two huge air compressors for the fog horn and an excellent model of the whole place at toddler height. Our three-year-old enjoyed having a turn on a morse code transmitter while we marvelled at the giant light bulbs from the tower. You can climb the tower to see the light and its old winding mechanism, and to enjoy the view which is superb on a clear day, but the steps are steep and rather perilous and little ones have to be carried.

There is a child-friendly restaurant serving light meals and teas, with colouring sheets and crayons for impatient customers. The gift shop has a good selection of books and cards on a nautical theme.

Fact File

- ADDRESS The Leas and Marsden Bay, South Shields, Tyne & Wear. Souter Lighthouse, Whitburn, South Shields
- TELEPHONE 0191 529 3161 (Lighthouse)
- DIRECTIONS 2 miles south of South Shields and 5 miles north of Sunderland on A183. From Newcastle take the Tyne Tunnel and follow brown signs to the Coast
- PUBLIC TRANSPORT Metro to South Shields town centre, buses to Whitburn
- DISTANCE 12 miles
- TRAVEL TIME 25 minutes
- OPENING March to November daily except Friday, 11.00am-5.00pm (Lighthouse)
- PRICES Adults £2.80, children £1.25, under-5's free (Lighthouse)
- RESTAURANT FACILITIES Yes
- NAPPY CHANGING FACILITIES No
- HIGH CHAIRS Yes
- DOGS No
- PUSHCHAIR-FRIENDLY Yes
- NEARBY Arbeia Roman Fort Museum (0191 456 1369)

Nature's World
With silver bells and cockle shells

THE INTRIGUING NAME, NATURE'S WORLD, DREW US TO EXPLORE, AND then to discover a place full of excitement. Here there are flower and vegetable gardens, a mini beast garden, a native butterfly house, willow maze, wildlife pond, a bee garden and a huge grass amphitheatre. Everywhere children are invited to touch, look, smell and explore. You'll find a 400m-long working model of the Tees too, and can walk alongside it from the miniature High Force waterfall, down past Barnard Castle, under the famous Middlesbrough Transporter Bridge (the real thing is clearly visible from the A19 on your way home) and right down to the Tees mouth. So even if you are not a particularly keen gardener, there is enough here to keep you busy all afternoon. One suggestion – though it is open all year round – if you visit in spring or summer you will catch the flowers at their prime and be more likely to find insects and birds around too.

> "Everywhere children are invited to touch, look, smell and explore"

The Centre is laid-out in a series of different interlinking gardens. Each one has a theme and though they are well-signed it is worth picking up a guide book and plan at the entrance, as this suggests a route and gives you a bit more detail. Early on you'll find the wildflower mountain, a small hill to scramble up, which gives a good view over the grounds and you can orientate yourselves from there.

If you're interested in Green issues this is the place for you. There is a huge composting display demonstrating the pros and cons of every single available composting bin. You can even go on a composting workshop!! While you investigate compost, your children will discover the wildlife corner nearby, where there are rabbits, guinea pigs, ducks and geese and Icarus, the amputee swan. There are also goats, chickens and turkeys and (to the delight of our animal lovers) a fur and foliage garden, where guinea pigs live in their own castle surrounded by a moat.

If you are not nervous, the bee garden with its glass-sided observation hive shows how bees fly in with their nectar and make honey. There are ordinary hives beside the trees at the edge of the garden and flowers planted specifically to attract the bees.

Following the trail past the Tees model head for the Mini Beast garden. This area consists of log and leaf piles, bits of carpet and dustbin lids, all intended to attract woodlice, centipedes, worms and spiders. Prepare to be there for a while as children lift things up and grub around finding little creatures. Leave them here while you explore the butterfly garden and tunnel next door, where you should see a variety of native butterflies and moths.

The final excitement of our visit was the Amnesty Willow Maze. Here we scurried up and down paths under arching willow trees, searching for the Candle of Hope in the centre. It is quite a difficult puzzle to solve unless you cheat, more so in spring when the trees are covered with new leaves. Being the first to reach the middle was certainly the highlight of our four-year-old son's day.

Back at the entrance there is a garden centre selling house and garden plants and organic vegetables. There is a tearoom, gift shop and a small children's play area too.

If you still have some energy drive on to Stewart Park, 10 minutes further on up the A174. Here there are acres of green to run around on and Highland cattle, llamas, deer, sheep and a pet's corner. Up at the top of the hill is the Captain Cooke birthplace museum, due to reopen in July 1997 after extensive refurbishment. We enjoyed our pre-refurbishment visit as it was on a quite a small scale with plenty of things for a young child. Look out for the wild banana tree and the giant cacti in the conservatory opposite the museum.

Fact File

- ADDRESS Nature's World, Ladgate Lane, Acklam, Middlesbrough
- TELEPHONE 01642 594895
- DIRECTIONS Tyne Tunnel then A19 towards Teeside. Take A174 off then B1380, following signs to Nature's World
- PUBLIC TRANSPORT Bus from Middlesbrough
- DISTANCE 40 miles
- TRAVEL TIME 50 minutes
- OPENING Daily 10.30am-5.00pm April to end September, 10.30am-4.30pm rest of year
- PRICES Adults £2.00, children £1.00, family £4.50
- RESTAURANT FACILITIES Yes
- NAPPY CHANGING FACILITIES No
- HIGH CHAIRS Yes
- DOGS Yes
- PUSHCHAIR-FRIENDLY Yes
- NEARBY Stewart Park and Captain Cooke birthplace museum (01642 813781)

Newby Hall

NEWBY HALL IS A REAL TREAT. NOT FAR OFF THE A1, IT OFFERS MORE than enough for a full day out. There is a splendid house with sumptuous decoration, 25 acres of varied gardens, a miniature railway, river trips, adventure gardens for children and a woodland walk. The gardens have been designed to bloom throughout the year, so there is as much to see on an autumn visit as in the spring and summer.

The Woodland Discovery Walk begins next to the car park, outside the entrance to the gardens. It is quite separate and worth doing first. It takes about half an hour and is a pleasant wander through woods and alongside a river, with little bridges, tree trunk seats and a number trail to keep small people amused. It is possible to take a buggy round. If you have brought a picnic you must eat it in the picnic area near the car park as picnics are not allowed in the gardens. This means you have to eat before going in unless you are prepared to drag everybody back to the car park half way through your visit – but at least it is one less bag to carry round.

You enter the gardens via the gift shop where you can buy a guide and map. We opted for the Adventure Gardens first and discovered a small exhibition of replica Crown Jewels en route, popular with our five-year-old who is heavily into kings and queens. The Adventure Gardens are great, though better for over-5's than under-5's. For three to five-year-olds there is a separate play area, for the very small there are swings, and ducks and swans up at one end of the pond, though you are asked not to feed them. Little ones need close supervision as the pond is not fenced. There are paddle boats on the pond which anyone can use but the weight limit is 10 stone, which may present a problem if you plan

> "A pleasant wander through woods and alongside a river, with little bridges, tree trunk seats and a number trail"

to take to the water with your child! A better option may be to take one of the river trips from the Newby Mooring – a picturesque glide along the River Ure with good views of the Hall and gardens (extra charge).

If you're there on a hot day, take swimming things as there is a paddling pool. It is knee deep for a five-year-old and looks wonderfully refreshing, parents must sit enviously by while kids splash and squeal.

The railway station is nearby and the train trip is great fun. It takes you up and down along the edge of the river, giving tantalising glimpses of the house, rock garden and grotto and fitting in a couple of bridges and a tunnel too. It lasts about 15 minutes and costs £1.00 per head.

The gardens themselves are beautiful with many parts which children can enjoy as well as parents. Particularly popular with our children were the Water Garden and the Rock Garden. They loved scurrying along the stony paths, winding amongst rocks and plants and discovering places – a stone bridge, a waterfall, a lily pond with a blue dragonfly and two terrapins swimming around. We enjoyed the Autumn Garden with its eucalyptus, fuchsia, hydrangeas and buddleias, and the magnificent herbaceous borders which run down from the house to the river. Some of the paths are tricky with a buggy but none is unmanageable.

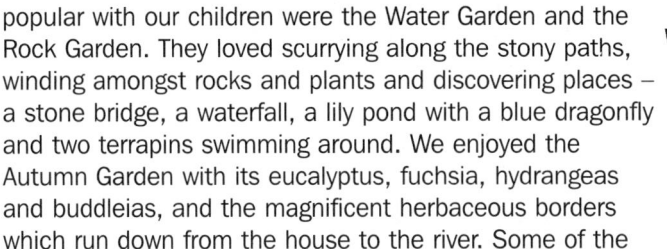

The house, more for adults than children, has been recently restored and has splendid ceilings and plasterwork. It contains some Chippendale furniture, tapestries and a gallery of classical statues.

The restaurant near the gift shop has an extensive hot and cold menu with children's dishes. There is also an ice cream kiosk near the station. If you're a gardener there is a plant shop in the car park with an interesting assortment of plants for sale.

Fact File

- ADDRESS Newby Hall, Skelton-on-Ure, Ripon, North Yorkshire
- TELEPHONE 01423 322583
- DIRECTIONS A1 south, onto the B6265 and through Skelton-on-Ure. Signposted
- PUBLIC TRANSPORT National Express bus to Ripon, local bus from Ripon to Newby Hall
- DISTANCE 75 miles
- TRAVEL TIME 1 hour 30 minutes
- OPENING 28 March to October daily (except Mondays), 11.00am-5.30pm. Open Bank Holiday Mondays
- PRICES Adults £4.00, children £2.70, under-4's free. Extra to enter Hall
- RESTAURANT FACILITIES Yes
- NAPPY CHANGING FACILITIES Yes
- HIGH CHAIRS Yes
- DOGS Only in picnic area
- PUSHCHAIR-FRIENDLY Yes
- NEARBY Fountains Abbey and Studley Royal Water Gardens (01765 608888)

Thornley Wood

IF YOU HAVEN'T ALREADY DISCOVERED THORNLEY WOOD THERE IS A TREAT in store. Here is a large woodland area with two ponds, meadows and a river. You can wander between mature oaks, pines and silver birch trees, watch for red squirrels from the observation hides and picnic with the butterflies on the tranquil meadow beside the river Derwent. Yet you are only minutes from the Metro Centre, and metres from the A1. There can be nowhere as close to the centre of Tyneside where you can escape from the bustle and noise and feel that you are in the heart of the country. Although the woods are beautiful in summer when you can loll around on a rug and dip your toes in the river, our family's favourite time is autumn, when the trees turn golden, the paths are edged with blackberries and mushrooms crop up near the river. Other friends like to visit in the winter and make straight for the observation hide. Food is put out regularly and you can be certain of seeing birds and perhaps even the above-mentioned squirrel.

You will find Thornley Wood on either side of the A694 from Swalwell to Rowlands Gill. On the left coming from Swalwell you will see signs for Thornley Woodland Centre. Here there is a small car park, toilets and an information centre.

The Centre is the starting point for three nature trails. Inside there is a display about Thornley wildlife and you can pick up leaflets

"There can be nowhere as close to the centre of Tyneside where you can escape from the bustle and noise"

and a map. The trails are marked by painted posts and you can easily find your way on your own. The short yellow route is the only one without steps and takes you through Paddock Hill Wood, up to a beech wood. At the bottom of this path you'll find the striding man statue, made from a large tree trunk.

The blue trail is best for young children, there is some climbing up and down steps, so it is not buggy-able, but the views are spectacular and well worth an extra piggy-back or shoulder ride. From the Centre walk along the edge of the Derwent valley on a board walk. The path splits soon after turning a corner and you can take left or right as both emerge at the same spot. The right-hand route takes you down the hill pretty steeply and can be slippery in the mud, but the views across the valley are wonderful. Down at the bottom you find yourselves on part of the Derwent Walk, an 11-mile trek along the bed of the old Derwent Valley Railway. Just along to the left there is the Nine Arches Viaduct, one of four along the Derwent Walk. Take the steps down again and you'll find the meadows, full of wild flowers in the summer and mushrooms in the autumn. These edge down to the river Derwent, slowly meandering its way to the Tyne at Swalwell. You may be lucky enough to see a kingfisher, a dipper or a heron, but the chances are that your noisy crew will frighten the wildlife away with their splashing and squealing.

The blue walk turns back on itself, retracing the same route. If you are feeling energetic, continue on the red route, following the river away from the viaduct and branching along the hill to Lockhaugh Farm. From there it's up to the first bridge, across this and then right to join the Derwent walk, back along to the steps at the foot of Paddock Hill Wood. This red trail is two and a half miles long and will take you at least an hour and a half.

The woods extend over the other side of the A694 too. Here there are other nature trails, including a green route which avoids steps. The observation hide is on this side of the road too, quite close to the start and overlooks a pond. The wood is crossed by Thornley Burn, which the path crosses on stepping stones (tricky after heavy rain). There is also Thornley Pond where you can find frogs, newts, dragonflies and damselflies.

Fact File

- ADDRESS Thornley Woodlands Centre, Rowlands Gill, Tyne & Wear
- TELEPHONE 01207 545212
- DIRECTIONS Go over the Scotswood Bridge, filter left and go over the next two roundabouts, heading for the A694. The woods are on either side of this road just beyond Winlaton Mill
- PUBLIC TRANSPORT Bus to Rowlands Gill
- DISTANCE 5 miles
- TRAVEL TIME 15 minutes
- OPENING Centre from 12 noon-5.00pm weekends and Bank Holidays, 12 noon-2.00pm weekdays
- PRICES Free
- RESTAURANT FACILITIES No
- NAPPY CHANGING FACILITIES No
- HIGH CHAIRS No
- DOGS Yes
- PUSHCHAIR-FRIENDLY No
- NEARBY National Trust's Gibside Chapel, a Palladian church and estate (01207 542255)

Wallington Hall

Mention Wallington to our children and they will talk about the dolls' houses, the frog spawn and the stone dragons' heads. My mother-in-law will enthuse about the walled garden and the fuchsia house. My own favourite is the woodland walk and the lake, so green and tranquil beneath the trees. Wallington has something to please everyone and can be visited often without becoming dull. Do choose a fine day though: the house is interesting but the grounds are the real pride and joy.

On arrival, walk up the path to the Clock Tower and go through the arch into the very large courtyard. Round the edge there is a small exhibition about the estate, a National Trust shop, a cafe, toilets and a room with carriages on show. In the middle there is a large expanse of lawn ideal for a bit of a run around after the car journey. Ball games are allowed so you can bring a football or a frisbee and work off some energy before setting off to walk. If it's a hot day it is a wonderful place to loll around and picnic. Before you head off though, don't miss the old mounting block on your right as you go through the wall towards the house: lots of fun to be had playing horses if parents are willing!

"**Winding paths through arches, under trees, beside little water channels and in and out of smartly trimmed hedges**"

The house is only open in the afternoons so walk first. Turn left through the wall and walk along the herbaceous border towards the road. The four stone dragon heads are on the right, great monsters for little ones to climb up and down, with a wide ditch between them and the road. Go across the road and through the gateway into the woods. The paths through the woods are delightful, winding beneath solid mature trees, amongst shrubs and wild flowers with alluring views of small lakes, distant hills, and a summer house. You emerge by a glassy green lake where a flock of ducks paddle around hoping for crusts. The wrought iron gate takes you into the walled garden.

For gardening enthusiasts this is a treat: there are well tended borders, an orchard, a terrace and a fabulous glasshouse full of conservatory plants in glorious bloom. There is a lot to explore too, winding paths that take you through arches, under trees, beside little water channels and in and out of smartly trimmed hedges. There are lots of seats so you can picnic, or just sit and admire the view while the kids keep appearing and reappearing and discovering new places. It's all manageable with a buggy.

Take the left hand path back to the House through the woods as it is the shortest and most direct. Neither pushchairs nor backpacks are allowed in the house: this is a firm rule and cannot be appealed against. Front sling baby carriers suitable for small babies are available. If you cannot bear the thought of going round with your toddler on the loose, don't go in at all, or take turns while the others sit on the lawn.

Having said that, Wallington has several special features that children love and it is a great shame to miss them. There is a marvellous collection of dolls' houses and a tiny playroom up a ladder (adults only allowed if accompanied by a child!), there are also toy soldier collections. Upstairs there is a nursery with toys and furniture and also a Museum of Curiosities with all sorts to see from stuffed birds to a doll's kitchen. Ask the guides to direct you straight to these rooms as there is little en route to interest young children. Other than these, don't miss the Central Hall, decorated with William Bell Scott's paintings from Northumberland's history. Kids love to see Grace Darling, St Cuthbert, the Vikings, the Romans, Bede and so on and telling the stories will keep you busy all the way home!

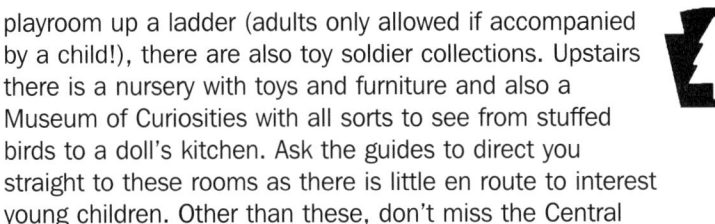

Back through the wall on the left the Clock Tower Restaurant serves good home-made fare, the service is pleasant and they have high chairs. Down below there is a smaller self-service cafe and a National Trust shop. Though not suitable for children, there is a summer season of outdoor Shakespeare plays at Wallington. You can bring a supper picnic then watch the play being performed in the gardens beside the house. Look out for details.

Fact File

- ADDRESS Wallington Hall, Cambo, near Morpeth, Northumberland
- TELEPHONE 01670 774283
- DIRECTIONS A696 and turn right onto the B6342 to Cambo
- PUBLIC TRANSPORT Bus in summer from Newcastle (0191 261 0610)
- DISTANCE 20 miles
- TRAVEL TIME 40 minutes
- OPENING Grounds all year daily during daylight hours. House from April to October 1.00pm-5.30pm or dusk, daily except Tuesday
- PRICES Grounds £2.80 adults, £1.40 children. House & grounds £4.80 adults, £2.40 children. Under-5's and National Trust members free
- RESTAURANT FACILITIES Yes
- NAPPY CHANGING FACILITIES Yes
- HIGH CHAIRS Yes
- DOGS Yes
- PUSHCHAIR-FRIENDLY Yes
- NEARBY Heighley Gate Garden Centre in Morpeth, with picnic and play area (01670 513416)

Somewhat Historical
Alnwick Castle

ALNWICK CASTLE OFFERS CHILDREN A GLIMPSE OF THE GLITTERING royal lifestyle which appears in their fairy tales. Its towers and walls stand tall and unsullied, while inside it's fit for a king. Sumptuous furniture, glowing oil paintings, and banks of porcelain fill the rooms with golden ceilings and gargantuan chandeliers shimmering above. Grand places and young children do not generally mix well, but take them into Alnwick Castle to see how the other half lives – you will have to keep them under control, but there aren't very many rooms and you can go round at your own pace! There is plenty of opportunity to let off steam outside in the grounds.

> "Our three-year-old couldn't tear himself away from a jewel-encrusted sword"

Children can chase around on the grass or play on the impressive line of cannons along the gun walk, while you sit and breathe in the peace of the surrounding countryside. Set right on the edge of the town, the castle overlooks the River Aln and offers beautiful views of the estate.

When you reach Alnwick follow the brown signs through the town to the castle. There are plenty of parking spaces along the road just outside. Even from there it is an impressive sight with its mighty stone walls and crenellated towers. Children will be intrigued by the stone figures standing guard on the roofs, silhouetted against the sky and looking like real soldiers. Inside the grounds you will discover a couple that have fallen down, so the children can have a good look: armless, legless and all.

Before going inside have a look at the splendid 19th century state coach on show and the museum of the Royal Northumberland Fusiliers. Any children interested in soldiers will enjoy the pictures, weapons and other memorabilia.

Head through the inner castle gateway but don't miss the dungeon on the way. Duck down a dark passageway on the right and you will emerge in a stone cell hung with shackles: children will shiver with delicious fear as they peer down through a grille in the middle of the floor and see straw and bones strewn grimly below.

Inside there is plenty to see and repeated warnings not to touch as everything is alarmed. If you go through at a reasonable pace with a firm grasp, it should be manageable. Again those keen on the military will be impressed with the Napoleonic arms in the Entrance Hall. Up the grand staircase you reach the family rooms. There are lots of things to catch the eye: our three-year-old couldn't tear himself away from a jewel-encrusted sword, while his sister was transfixed by the crystal chandeliers sparkling above each room. We all liked the large collection of hand-crafted shepherds crooks, their hooks carved from horn into fishes, ducks, foxes, a woodpecker and many other birds and beasts.

Coming outside again there is a small adventure playground suitable for over-4's. Inside the castle walls on the opposite side are two small museums of antiquities, but with little to interest young children. Head instead for the Gun Walk and its magnificent collection of 15 cannons which provide a much more exciting adventure playground.

There is a cafe in the castle serving light lunches, cakes and drinks. If you don't fancy eating there, Alnwick has plenty of pubs offering bar meals. There's a shop next to the cafe selling cards, books and gifts. They do a good line in model soldiers for those with pocket money to spend.

Fact File

- ADDRESS Alnwick Castle, Alnwick, Northumberland
- TELEPHONE 01665 510777
- DIRECTIONS A1 north to Alnwick. Follow signs to castle
- PUBLIC TRANSPORT Northumbria 501 bus from Berwick to Alnwick has connection from Newcastle
- DISTANCE 31 miles
- TRAVEL TIME 50 minutes
- OPENING Daily, except Fridays, 11.00am-5.00pm, Good Friday to end September
- PRICES Castle & Grounds £5.75 adults, £3.50 children, family £13.00. Grounds only £4.00. Under-5's free
- RESTAURANT FACILITIES Yes
- NAPPY CHANGING FACILITIES Yes
- HIGH CHAIRS Yes
- DOGS No
- PUSHCHAIR-FRIENDLY Yes
- NEARBY Alnmouth beach and town, for a beautiful sandy beach, walks and pleasant pubs and cafes

Bamburgh Castle

A dungeon horrible, on all sides round . . .

ONE OF THE MOST SPECTACULAR CASTLES IN BRITAIN, BAMBURGH should not be missed. Set on a huge rocky outcrop overlooking the North sea, it has fabulous views of Holy Island, the Farne Islands and Dunstanburgh, and to the west the Cheviot Hills. Everything in a child's imagined castle is here: a keep, turrets, cannons on the ramparts, suits of armour, shields and swords, rich tapestries and carpets and best of all, a dungeon full of horrors. Added to all this, the beach just below the castle is a glorious stretch of fine golden sand with rock pools at the northern end and sand dunes to the south.

A fortress has been standing on the same site since Norman times, but the castle's heyday was in the Middle Ages, when kings of England used Bamburgh as a stronghold against the Scots for 400 years. The castle was rescued from the decline suffered by many other such buildings by Lord Armstrong who bought the castle at the beginning of this century and set about restoring it to its former glory. This means that the castle looks very much intact with vast thick walls, towers, an imposing Norman keep and splendid public rooms inside.

> **"Everything in a child's imagined castle is here"**

The castle dominates the village and signs to the car park are clearly marked. As soon as you enter and climb up onto the battlements you find the line of cannons. Our children love to clamber on these, gaze out over the ocean and fire at passing pirates. Note that you are not allowed to picnic within the grounds, so save your lunch for the beach or eat in the Clock Tower Tea Rooms inside which have sandwiches, drinks and homemade cakes at reasonable prices.

☞ Going round the inside will probably take about 45 minutes. There are 16 rooms of varying interest to children, some are set out in museum style, others as period rooms. Some exhibits are alarmed and buzz if touched so you need to supervise your kids closely. Our family favourites are the wooden bicycle and the sedan chair in the Crewe Museum Room, the suits of armour in the splendid King's Hall, closely followed by the armoury. The dungeons, the last rooms you come to, are fairly explicit, showing lifelike figures in chains with blood and gore dripping from their brows. You can miss them completely if you think it's too scary.

In the grounds there is The Armstrong Museum of Victorian Industrial Archeology, not of great interest to young children though they may like the model ship and tank. Instead why not head for the beach – take the right turn after the cricket pitch below the castle. This is known as The Wynding and takes you out to the top of the beach. You can park at the side of the road and it's a short clamber down to the sand below.

There is another small museum in Bamburgh, The Grace Darling Museum, opposite the church at the other end of the street from the castle. This contains the boat in which Grace and her father rowed to rescue the drowning sailors and pictures, books and other memorabilia to bring the story to life. Bamburgh is full of pubs and tea shops; Blacketts at the top does children's meals and has high chairs. There is also a small deli with a good range of bread, cheese and cold meat, which is open on Sundays in season.

Fact File

- ADDRESS Bamburgh Castle, Bamburgh, Northumberland
- TELEPHONE 01669 621555
- DIRECTIONS A1 north, then the B1341 to Bamburgh
- PUBLIC TRANSPORT Bus 501 direct Newcastle to Bamburgh
- DISTANCE 50 miles
- TRAVEL TIME 1 hour
- OPENING Daily 11.00am-5.00pm Easter to end of October. Last admission 30 minutes before closing
- PRICES Adults £3.50, children £1.50, under-7's free
- RESTAURANT FACILITIES Yes
- NAPPY CHANGING FACILITIES Yes
- HIGH CHAIRS Yes
- DOGS No
- PUSHCHAIR-FRIENDLY Yes, some steps
- NEARBY Grace Darling Museum in Bamburgh

Beamish

BEAMISH IS AS FAR AWAY FROM A TRADITIONAL MUSEUM AS YOU CAN imagine. It is open air, huge and immediate. There are no glass cases, stuffed birds or buttons to push, instead you explore buildings that have been rescued from all over the North East and rebuilt on the site. Each has been authentically furnished in pre-1914 style with great attention to detail, and many are staffed with people acting in role as farmers, miners, and shopkeepers whose job is to chat to you and bring the place to life. With few notices and information boards, the buildings and staff speak for themselves, and it is a vivid experience even for small children.

You may need more than one visit, as there is so much to see. Currently there is a farm, a drift mine, a colliery, a street, a manor house, a school, a chapel, a station and a fairground. The trams linking each area can be boarded at any stop. These are a highlight for our kids who dash upstairs to find a place on the open top deck, regardless of the wind chill factor. From there they point out their favourite spots and wave to the lowly pedestrians! If you want to visit the mine it's a good idea to go straight there as it can get quite busy. There are guided tours taking you down to the coal face. Definitely one to avoid if you get claustrophobic as adults spend most of the time crouching down. Children love it as they can stand upright and everyone gets to wear a hard hat. They chatter on about the seven dwarfs while you hear about the hardships the miners endured.

> "Children like playing with the traditional iron hoops in the playground"

The fairground on the events field is a must, although you have to pay extra. There are swingboats, flying chairs, a real old carousel and a coconut shy. There are often special events at weekends too, such as veteran car and motor-cycle rallies,north-country wrestling and whippet racing.

The town is typical of a small North East market town in 1913 and features a pub, a park, a garage, a Co-op, a row of terraced houses and some other shops. Particularly popular is the sweet shop where they make boiled sweets and rock in the back room. You can buy a bag of barley sugar or humbugs to suck on your way round. The Co-op is a fascinating shop to browse in, looking at all the old-fashioned goods and chatting to the shop-keepers. Do check out the overhead Heath Robinson contraption which delivers bills to the cash office. All along the street you hear cries of "Oh look! We used to have one of those!" and "Do you remember them?" – one of the best things about Beamish for adults is spotting things you remember from childhood or from your grandmother's house.

Above the Co-op there are the Dainty Diner Tearooms serving hot and cold meals, snacks, drinks and cakes. You have to carry your buggy up, but there are high chairs. You can also buy drinks and sandwiches in the pub and children are welcome. Have a quick look in the stables behind the pub where the two dray horses live; there is a great collection of tack and brasses. If the horses are not inside they will be out and about in the museum somewhere.

Steam train lovers shouldn't miss the station, with the signal box where the signal man shows you how to operate the levers. The loco stands outside in the station yard and can be explored too. If it's a chilly day make a pit-stop in the Ladies' Waiting Room where there's usually a warm fire going.

Onward to the farm where there's a good collection of animals, an exhibition of old machinery and a farmhouse where you'll find the farmer and his wife. She is busy baking while he sits by the range telling you about the days of privies and tin baths. In the dairy watch cheese making, (which you can buy from the shop) and outside there is a blacksmith at work. There is a small kiosk in the farm area selling hot snacks, but this is only open at weekends.

The school is another favourite spot with our children. They like playing with the traditional iron hoops in the playground and having a scribble on the old slates, meanwhile we're back down memory lane in the classroom recalling our own primary school days.

A recent building to open is Pockerley Manor Farm, both older and grander than most of the other buildings in the museum. It's the local squire's house and is furnished accordingly, with an 'upstairs-downstairs' feel, grand bedrooms on the one hand and poky servants' quarters on the other. There are demonstrations of calligraphy and candle making. Be warned – it is rather dark and shadowy and can be scary. There are stables and horses outside and a terraced garden.

If you've managed to take in even half of the museum you will be exhausted by the time you reach the exit. A cup of tea is again at hand in the coffee shop and there is a large shop to visit too with cards, books, toys and a lot of heritage industry paraphernalia.

Fact File

- ADDRESS Beamish Museum, Beamish, Stanley, County Durham
- TELEPHONE 01207 231811
- DIRECTIONS A1(M) south to Chester-le-Street exit. Clearly signposted
- PUBLIC TRANSPORT Bus from Newcastle (Northern/Classic 709), or Durham (Diamond 720 and X79)
- DISTANCE 10 miles
- TRAVEL TIME 30 minutes
- OPENING Daily 10.00am-5.00pm 22 March to 26 October. Last admission 4.00pm. Daily, except Mondays and Friday, 10.00am-4.00pm the rest of the year with town and tram only
- PRICES Adults £7.99 (school holidays), £6.99 (summer), £2.99 (winter). Children £4.99 all year, except £1.99 in winter. Under-5's free
- RESTAURANT FACILITIES Yes
- NAPPY CHANGING FACILITIES Yes
- HIGH CHAIRS Yes
- DOGS No
- PUSHCHAIR-FRIENDLY Yes
- NEARBY Derwent Walk Country Park, walk along former railway from Swalwell to Consett. Picnic areas, woodland and visitor centres

Bede's World

A MUSEUM ABOUT THE LIFE AND TIMES OF THE VENERABLE BEDE MAY not sound like the most gripping of days out with a young family, but this is a museum with a difference. Here you can explore an Anglo-Saxon house, meet wild pigs and shaggy black oxen (almost the same breeds as those living in the Middle Ages), try on a hand-woven shirt and listen to Latin being spoken. Bede's World is very much an experience and has something to offer any-aged visitor. It is partly an open air museum though, so it would be best to visit on a dry day.

Inside the museum (a striking new building designed with an open courtyard) there is an exhibition about the Venerable Bede and about Northumbria in Bede's time. There are pictures, artefacts and a fair bit for adults to read, but of far greater interest for children is the handling collection – a set of drawers containing clothes which can be tried on, and other 'Anglo-Saxon' items such as a spindle and a bone spoon. Ours also enjoyed picking up the telephones and listening to the spoken Latin and old Welsh, although the attraction was more the technology than the history! Before you go outside do look for the Celtic Cross perched on the bank at the far end. It gives a dramatic silhouette and is something for children to find again later.

"Ours kids enjoyed listening to the spoken Latin and old Welsh"

The farm provides a good contrast. Here you'll find an experimental reconstruction of an Anglo-Saxon farm, with native breeds of sheep, ducks, geese and chickens all living in small fields, bordered by woven hazel fences. Oxen are used to plough the fields where ancient strains of wheat are grown. Most popular with our three though, were the two wild pigs with their hairy coats, sharp teeth and long snouts. Note the warnings about bites and make sure little fingers are kept well away.

☞ Around the edge of the farm there are reconstructions of timber huts and halls, such as Anglo-Saxon people might have lived in. There are plans to develop this further and this part of the museum will clearly have more to show in the future. Look out for the stream, cleverly landscaped through the farm from a reed bed at the top to a pond with a ford at the bottom. It is a pleasant walk around, with scope for the children to race round and explore, and everywhere is passable with a buggy (including a ford by-pass). There are good views of the river Tyne and the river Don. (The museum overlooks the port of Tyne and Nissan's export terminal and happy times may be spent by small people watching cranes at work and rows and rows of shining new cars.)

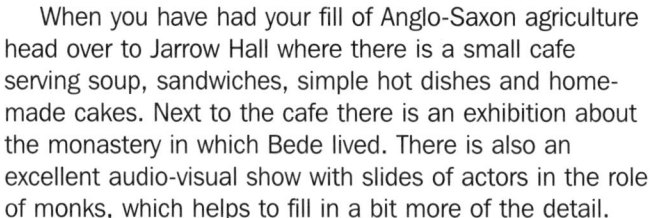

When you have had your fill of Anglo-Saxon agriculture head over to Jarrow Hall where there is a small cafe serving soup, sandwiches, simple hot dishes and home-made cakes. Next to the cafe there is an exhibition about the monastery in which Bede lived. There is also an excellent audio-visual show with slides of actors in the role of monks, which helps to fill in a bit more of the detail.

There are swings and a slide outside the Hall and a green for chasing about or kicking a ball. After a breather you might like to visit St Paul's church, the only surviving part of the original 7th century monastery. Outside you can also explore the monastic ruins. There is a gift shop in the church and one back at the museum, which has some good Celtic pictures, posters and colouring books.

Fact File

- ADDRESS Bede's World, Church Bank, Jarrow, Tyne & Wear
- TELEPHONE 0191 489 2106
- DIRECTIONS Tyne Tunnel from Newcastle, second exit, follow signs to museum
- PUBLIC TRANSPORT Bede and Jarrow metro stations. Bus services 526 and 527
- DISTANCE 10 miles
- TRAVEL TIME 20 minutes
- OPENING 10.00am-5.30pm Tuesday-Saturday and Bank Holidays, 2.30pm-5.30pm Sunday from April to October. From November to March 11.00am-4.30pm Tuesday-Saturday, and 2.30pm-5.30 Sunday
- PRICES Adults £2.50, children £1.25, under-5's free, family £6.00
- RESTAURANT FACILITIES Yes
- NAPPY CHANGING FACILITIES Yes
- HIGH CHAIRS Yes
- DOGS Yes
- PUSHCHAIR-FRIENDLY Yes
- NEARBY South Shields beach, park and amusements

Durham Cathedral

A DAY OUT WITH CHILDREN IN A CHURCH DOESN'T SOUND LIKE AN instant vote-winner, but Durham Cathedral may be the notable exception. It is a wonderful building, quite the tallest, longest, most echoey place a small child has ever been in. The mighty pillars amaze, the stained glass windows delight, the lofty vaulted roof may even silence a child, momentarily at least, while the experience is just as awe-inspiring for a parent.

The cathedral towers above the town and is instantly identifiable from any direction. Arriving by train it is a 15-minute walk to the town centre down a steep but buggy-able path. By car you can park in the multi-storey car park at Old Elvet. Begin your visit with a walk along the riverside, you can get down at Framwellgate Bridge or Old Elvet Bridge, immediately outside the car park. There are rowing boats for hire here so if you've enough adults and it's a sunny day why not take to the water?

"Quite the tallest, longest, most echoey place a small child has ever been in"

The riverside path is delightful, passing through leafy tree tunnels and alongside ducks and the odd rowboat or coxed four during University term-time. It's about half a mile and flat enough for a pushchair though you may need a hand getting down in the first place. Take the path up the hill just by the archaeological museum and you will emerge on the Palace Green near the cathedral entrance.

Once inside you can buy a pamphlet to guide you round or just wander and get a feel for the place. Favourites with our children are the Mark Angus stained glass window west of the North Door with its tremendous purples and crimsons which flood across the aisle on a sunny day, the stone lions below the pulpit and the intriguing wooden clock to the north of the crossing. Our three-year-old is also very taken with the effigies on the various tombs.

HEINZ GUIDE TO DAYS OUT WITH KIDS **97**

We have never attempted to climb the tower (325 steps are a bit too many for a piggyback) but the view over County Durham is reputed to be tremendous. The Treasury in the undercroft is worth a look though. The gleaming gold and silver plate look so opulent and everyone loves to have a hold of the lion's head knocker. During the summer you will find the 'Building the Church' exhibition in the crypt which explains how buildings such as Durham Cathedral were built.

The toilets, shop and cafe are next door. The cafe is self-service and has hot and cold meals, snacks and drinks. If the kids are ready to let off steam, head for the Botanical Gardens. These are on Hollingside Lane off South Road, about a mile from the centre. Here you can picnic or eat in their cheap and cheerful cafe. Away from the hustle and bustle of town the gardens are a great place to race and chase and play hide and seek. There is a tropical house and a cactus house, mature woods, a river, a pond and the Prince Bishops Garden where you come face to face with great figures from Durham's history.

Fact File

- ADDRESS Durham Cathedral, Palace Green, Durham, County Durham
- TELEPHONE 0191 386 4266 (Chapter Office)
- DIRECTIONS Signposted off the A1. Once in town you can't miss it
- PUBLIC TRANSPORT Regular train services from Newcastle
- DISTANCE 20 miles
- TRAVEL TIME 30 minutes
- OPENING 7.15am-8.00pm May to September, 7.15am-6.00pm October to April. Tower 9.30am-4.00pm, closed Sundays and during services. Treasury 10.00am-4.30pm Monday-Saturday, 2.00pm-4.30pm Sunday
- PRICES Cathedral is free though donations gratefully received. Tower £2.00 adults, £1.00 children. Treasury £1.00 adults, 50p children. Under-4's free
- RESTAURANT FACILITIES Yes
- NAPPY CHANGING FACILITIES Yes
- HIGH CHAIRS Yes
- DOGS No
- PUSHCHAIR-FRIENDLY Yes
- NEARBY Durham Botanical Gardens (0191 374 2670)

Hartlepool Historic Quay

Fifteen men on a dead man's chest
Yo ho ho and a bottle of rum!

THIS IS A MUSEUM WITH A DIFFERENCE. IT IS A RECONSTRUCTION OF AN entire 18th century seaport, complete with market, shops, prison, traditional playground and a whole collection of barrels, ropes, crates and piles of cannon balls at the water's edge. The only things missing are the ships themselves, though HMS Trincomalee, Britain's oldest floating warship, is moored at Jackson Dock, next to the museum and can be visited if you've got the energy after a day at the Quay.

There's plenty to see inside as well as out and you'll still enjoy it if it's wet. There are two film shows to watch and also Fighting Ships, an extraordinary tour through a series of life-sized tableaux depicting the captain and crew of the fighting frigate Prosperity. They come to life as you pass with the help of lights and sound effects and tell you about the way they live. The grand finale is a simulated sea battle with cannons firing, clouds of smoke, screams, flashes and explosions. The realistic models (including ship's surgeon with a saw in hand and a bucket of severed limbs) and the loud noises may be too much for some children, especially toddlers. You'll know if your child is likely to cope (five-year-olds and over would probably be excited rather than frightened), but if you're unsure leave it until last. There are plenty of other things to see and do even if you miss Fighting Ships altogether.

> **"Try your hand at skittles, quoits, ninepins or fishing for frenchies!"**

Each of the shops is staffed with lifelike models and has a soundtrack running, with one of the characters explaining the scene. The words go over children's heads but there are all sorts of things to catch the eye and some hands-on activities inside the shops. In Cornelius Mumford's Printers' shop for instance, there are ink stamps and paper to experiment with, while in the naval architect's office there is a stack of wooden crates containing larger-than-life stowaways of the mini-beastie variety. Children love opening the doors and discovering spiders, scorpions, mice, tapeworms and so on. Here all the hardships and violence of 18th century life are clearly shown, from the burns on the powder monkeys' arms, to the weevil-infested ships' biscuits, and we came out feeling very thankful for having been born in the 20th century.

Behind the shops there are several other galleries with models, pictures and old weapons. The Cutting Edge, behind the swordsmiths, displays old swords and has a tableau of a battle scene on deck. This time it is on a miniature scale and was very popular with our three-year-old, who pressed the button at least four times and stood captivated as the sound effects and subtle lighting brought the scene alive. He also enjoyed the model fighting ship in the India room with buttons to press showing activities on each of the different decks. Meanwhile older children were experimenting with a computer programme which told them about the members of the ship's crew.

Outside on the quayside there is Skittle Square, a playground with traditional children's games to have a go at. Since the square is well-fenced in and completely safe for little ones, it provides a good break for everyone and it certainly isn't only the children keen to try their hand at skittles, quoits, ninepins or fishing for frenchies! Further along the quay you find Hartness Market with stalls for cheese and dried and preserved meat, baskets, ropes, flour and so on. There is a large gift shop in the centre of the quayside where you can buy all those vital pirate accessories such as hooks, daggers, eye patches and hats; it also sells traditional wooden toys, cards, books and ornaments. The Quayside Coffee Shop just next door serves sandwiches, cakes, ices and a few hot meals. It has a couple of highchairs.

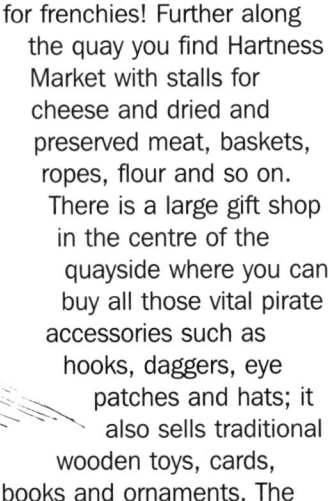

Fact File

- ADDRESS Hartlepool Historic Quay, Hartlepool Marina, Hartlepool, Cleveland
- TELEPHONE 01429 860888
- DIRECTIONS A19 south, then the A179 to Hartlepool. Follow blue RAC signs to Historic Quay
- PUBLIC TRANSPORT Bus from Newcastle to Hartlepool. Alight at Grand Hotel, and it's a 10-minute walk
- DISTANCE 35 miles
- TRAVEL TIME 45 minutes
- OPENING Daily 10.00am-7.00pm (summer and school holidays), 5.00pm (other times). Last admission 2 hours earlier
- PRICES Adults £4.95, children £2.50, under-5's free, family £13.00
- RESTAURANT FACILITIES Yes
- NAPPY CHANGING FACILITIES Yes
- HIGH CHAIRS Yes
- DOGS No
- PUSHCHAIR-FRIENDLY Yes
- NEARBY HMS Trincomalee (01429 223193) for guided tours inside ship

Housesteads Fort & Hadrian's Wall

THIS IS A TRIP FOR A CRISP CLEAR DAY, WINTER OR SUMMER. THE drive from Chollerford is fabulous as the Roman Road (B6318) rolls west like a ribbon laid over the contours of the hills. Alongside you catch glimpses of the remains of Hadrian's Wall and beyond that increasingly wild border country. Standing on a stone look-out post at Housesteads Fort the view stretches for miles and you can understand why Emperor Hadrian chose such a vantage point for his frontier, though winters must have been bleak. The kids meanwhile need little encouragement

> "A maze of little rooms to explore, nooks and crannies to squeeze through and grassy banks to roll down"

in such a dramatic place to launch into imaginary worlds of soldiers and savages. A word of advice – don't visit Housesteads on a wet or windy day: it is very exposed and can be bitterly cold. Even on a fine day it may be pretty chilly, so go well prepared as cold children are miserable companions.

The National Trust owns about six miles of the Wall from Steel Rigg to Housesteads, including the Fort. The car park for Housesteads is on the right immediately next to the B6318 about seven miles beyond Chollerford; here is a small information centre, toilets and refreshment counter. The information centre is free and has a particularly good model of the Wall in three different periods: being built, defended and falling into ruins. The display case is at toddler height and includes a number of figures which help to bring it to life. There is also a shop in the centre with National Trust goodies and a fine selection of books on Roman history, many for children.

The museum, fort and Wall are all on the next ridge, a 10-minute walk down and up a small valley. The path is stony and quite steep, it would be difficult with a buggy and the fort even more tricky to negotiate, so it's better to bring a backpack if you can. Buy tickets for the fort in the museum entrance and have look at the life-size Roman soldier and the model of the fort in Roman times. Of more interest to our kids though were the chain-mail curtains and the prints of Roman life, particularly the one of the latrines.

The fort itself is the best preserved of all the Roman Wall forts, although few of the walls stand higher than a foot. It has been substantially excavated and there are information boards and pictures to help you envisage it as it must have been once. The commandant's house in the centre is interesting, particularly the room full of pillars which formed part of the central heating system for the house. Next to it there is a hospital and elsewhere a granary, a kiln and the remains of soldiers' barracks. We searched for the latrines and found them in the south east corner, but to the children's disappointment the rows of seats had gone and most of the floor, so they couldn't try them out!

To young children the fort is a very exciting adventure playground, with a maze of little rooms to explore, nooks and crannies to squeeze through and grassy banks to roll down. There are sheep in the surrounding fields and a fair spread of droppings even within the fort. You can get onto the Roman Wall here and walk along a bit. The section west of Housesteads is the most spectacular for walking with superb views. It is rough going though with lots of steps and huffing and puffing up and down.

Once you've had your fill of Roman history there are any number of small villages with pleasant pubs nearby. Our favourite is The Hadrian in Wall which welcomes children, there's also The George at Chollerford which is very popular. If you're interested in gardening don't miss Hexham Herbs, a walled garden centre on the right, half way back from Housesteads to Chollerford; it is a lovely place for a wander around and houses the national collection of thyme. Finally if the kids need a run around, Tyne Green, on your right across the river into Hexham has a good playground and you can walk along a path by the river. There are toilets and a small cafe down there too.

Fact File

- ADDRESS Housesteads Fort, Bardon Mill, Hexham, Northumberland
- TELEPHONE 01434 344363
- DIRECTIONS A69 west from Newcastle, then A6079 and B6318 (the Roman Road) to Housesteads
- PUBLIC TRANSPORT Buses available in summer (01434 605225)
- DISTANCE 35 miles
- TRAVEL TIME 45 minutes
- OPENING Daily 10.00am-6.00pm or dusk in winter
- PRICES Adults £2.50, children £1.30, under-5's free. Free to National Trust and English Heritage members
- RESTAURANT FACILITIES Yes
- NAPPY CHANGING FACILITIES No
- HIGH CHAIRS No
- DOGS Yes
- PUSHCHAIR-FRIENDLY No
- NEARBY Hexham is a pleasant market town with Abbey and riverside park

Richmond Castle & Town

RICHMOND IS AN OLD MARKET TOWN ON THE BANKS OF THE RIVER Swale, right on the edge of the high dales and standing at the entrance to Swaledale. It offers a chance to walk along the river to the falls and enjoy some spectacular views without leaving town. There is the castle to visit, its tower and high walls rising impressively above the town and its green rolling grounds an irresistible spot for chasing around and playing hide and seek. Then there is the town itself, with steep cobbled streets, little pathways and shortcuts winding up to the huge open market place, where everyone sits to watch the world go by.

There are three car parks, a free one near the swimming pool, a short-stay one by the falls and a long-stay one next to the sports field. At the first you can spread out your rug and picnic on the Batts, a large grassy area above the river bank, or you can perch yourselves on the pebbly beach right at the water's edge. The kids can potter about throwing stones into the water and building dams while you enjoy the peace broken only by the church bells chiming the hour. If you visit in autumn the trees are a treat, mature oak, sycamore and chestnut turning orange and gold and dropping acorns, helicopter seeds and glossy conkers. After the stripped trees of the city, our children could not believe their luck finding piles of virgin conkers and we returned home with everyone's pockets full.

"Plenty to explore within the castle walls and grassy slopes to roll down"

If you stroll along the river for half an hour away from the town you will come to the remains of Easby Abbey, crumbling ruins in a tranquil spot. Walking the other way you reach the River Swale Falls, where the river tumbles

☞

over steep shelves of rocks, rushing in several courses down to the stones below. There are toilets in the car park above the falls and a kiosk selling ices, drinks and snacks. The Castle is a short walk from there.

Richmond Castle towers above the town and river, was built in 1071 as a Norman stronghold, and is mentioned in the Domesday Book. The great Keep was added a century later and served as a northern fortress throughout the Middle Ages. The Keep is 100' high and commands a marvellous view. It is rather a struggle clambering up the stone stairs but worth it for the view over the dales and the town. Children love peering over the parapet and climbing into the corner towers. They are reasonably safe as the walls are high. You can point out the outline on the grass left by the 19th century barracks which were built in the inner court but have since been demolished. You can also see how the market place echoes the shape of the outer court of the castle.

There is plenty to explore within the castle walls, the Great Hall, Robin Hood Tower, the Solar, and grassy slopes to roll down. It's a perfect place for toddlers as it is enclosed but offers them an enormous space to rush around in without getting lost. The castle is owned by English Heritage and there is a programme of special events from May to August, in 1997 ranging from Vikings to Scottish Pipes and King Arthur to Morris Men.

Down in the market place and ready for refreshment, you will be spoiled for choice. Our favourite is the Castle Hill Restaurant and Tearoom, set slightly back on the river side of the square. They serve good, wholesome Yorkshire fare with children's meals and home-made cakes. If you'd rather eat at a pub, the Town Hall Hotel serves High-Tea-type food such as toasties, filled baked potatoes and giant Yorkshire puds with gravy from 3.00pm until 7.00pm. Children are welcome at both these places.

Fact File

- ADDRESS Richmond Castle, Richmond, N. Yorkshire
- TELEPHONE 01748 822493
- DIRECTIONS A1 south to Scotch Corner, A6108 to Richmond
- PUBLIC TRANSPORT Train to Darlington from Newcastle. Bus from there (01325 468771)
- DISTANCE 50 miles
- TRAVEL TIME 1 hour
- OPENING Daily all year, 10.00am-6.00pm, or to 4.00pm in winter. Closed for lunch 1.00pm-2.00pm in winter
- PRICES Adults £1.80, children 90p. Under-5's and English Heritage members free
- RESTAURANT FACILITIES Yes
- NAPPY CHANGING FACILITIES No
- HIGH CHAIRS Some restaurants
- DOGS Yes
- PUSHCHAIR-FRIENDLY Yes
- NEARBY Darlington Railway Centre (01325 460532), a restored station with exhibition including Stephenson's Locomotion

Warkworth Castle

ONE OF OUR FAVOURITE DAYS OUT, WARKWORTH HAS SOMETHING FOR everyone and takes some beating on a sunny day. A real Medieval castle with towers to climb, huge echoing stone rooms to visit and a grassy moat to roll up and down. Then there is the river to walk along with rowing boats for hire and a ferry across to the old Hermitage. The town itself has pleasant bookshops and arty-crafty shops, as well as a number of friendly pubs and teashops; and finally just north of town, there's the beach – a wide stretch of sand backed by dunes. In fact there's almost more than enough for one day, especially if you fit in tea at The Greenhouse, the cafe right in the middle of town. The home-made cakes there are superb and you can read the papers (provided) while the kids sit and draw at the small blackboard-topped tables.

The castle dominates the town, standing on an earth mound with a deep ditch around it. In spring this is covered in daffodils and looks lovely; in summer the banks are grassed and quite irresistible to children who tear up and come hurtling down, time and time again. Inside the castle walls there's plenty of space to run around in too, as well as a complicated tangle of ruins. Warkworth is really two castles, an early Medieval one built over several centuries and now standing in ruins and the great keep: built in the fourteenth century and still in good repair. While the ruins invite plenty of climbing and jumping off, the keep is better for exploring and playing 'Let's Pretend'. The rooms are still intact and pictures help you imagine them as they once were – an ox roasting over the mighty kitchen fire, a banquet in the Great Hall with musicians playing in the balcony above, rich tapestries hanging in the Percy family room next door. While you

> "The banks are grassed and quite irresistible to children who tear up and come hurtling down"

muse, your children will be disappearing down passageways and up staircases; discovering the wine cellar and the pantry. Follow them – it is reasonably safe but there is the odd spot where the floor is missing . . . !

For a real feel of the castle in historic times visit on one of the special event days (May Bank holiday weekends and most weekends during the summer holidays). There is a range of Medieval and Viking entertainment on offer, with lots of audience participation, dancing, children's games to join in, informal talks, archery and music.

☞ When you have had enough of history, go down to the river and wander along under the trees beside the gently flowing River Coquet. Leave your car in the castle car park, turn right over the drawbridge and go down the flight of steps by the fence. The path at the bottom leads on down to the river, emerging on the bank at the boat hire spot. If you prefer to walk, it is a delightful amble half a mile down to the spot opposite the Hermitage (check at the castle ticket office for opening hours). If it is open there will be a boat available to ferry you across, then it is a short walk along to the stone steps up to the Hermitage, a series of rooms cut into the rock where hermits once lived and prayed. To an adult it seems an austere yet moving place, to a child it is a fairytale cavern. As you walk back towards the town the views of the castle are wonderful.

If you'd prefer the sea to the river, drive down through the town, veer right with the main road and cross the fine stone bridge, take the next turning on the right and follow this narrow road down to a car park. The beach is a five-minute walk on a path that crosses a golf course. It is a beautiful sweep of sand and is never crowded. Take all your supplies with you as there is nothing there, though there are public toilets in the car park.

Fact File

- ADDRESS Warkworth Castle, Warkworth, Northumberland
- TELEPHONE 01665 711423
- DIRECTIONS A189 north from Newcastle, A1068 to Warkworth
- PUBLIC TRANSPORT Northumbria X18 Newcastle to Alnwick bus (01670 533128)
- DISTANCE 31 miles
- TRAVEL TIME 45 minutes
- OPENING Daily 10.00am-6.00pm (summer), 4.00pm (winter)
- PRICES Adults £2.20, children £1.10, under-5's free
- RESTAURANT FACILITIES In Warkworth
- NAPPY CHANGING FACILITIES No
- HIGH CHAIRS In Warkworth
- DOGS Yes
- PUSHCHAIR-FRIENDLY Yes
- NEARBY Warkworth Beach or Hermitage

Up, Down, There & Back
Heatherslaw Railway

THIS IS A GREAT LITTLE RAILWAY! IF YOU GET THE TIMING RIGHT YOU WILL be able to have a delightful train ride, a peaceful picnic in the shadow of a ruined castle, a dip in the river and a tour round a working flour mill. There's history, engineering, flora, fauna, and plenty of good old messing about near water.

But first the train ride. Heatherslaw Light Railway is a mile and three quarter piece of track connecting Heatherslaw to Etal. It is a narrow gauge line with a miniature steam train, The Lady Augusta. Shiny and noisy enough to impress, without frightening the more timid would-be engine drivers, it has the best whistle of all the trains we've been on.

> "The train hugs the bank of the river Till, so close you could almost tickle a trout as you ride"

Start the day at Heatherslaw, with a look at the Railway room. This is run by a group of model railway enthusiasts and if you are lucky enough to catch any of them there (usually Thursdays and Saturdays) then you're in for fun. They have two of the most impressive model railway layouts you can imagine. Kids are allowed to try their skill at manoeuvring various trains, picking up extra wagons, firing the missile launcher or simply driving the Hornby trains around the track. There are crayons and paper for drawings, and children are invited to compose poems for an annual competition.

After that it's "all aboard" for the 20-minute ride up to Etal. No uniforms or flag-waving here and the diddy little carriages are rather spartan, some even open-sided, but their very smallness makes the children feel that they belong to them, not the adults!

The train runs at a gentle jogging speed with an authentic 'Jicketty can' as it trundles along. It hugs the bank of the river Till, so close you could almost tickle a trout as you ride. You wind in and out of the reeds and bushes, and for the sharp-eyed there are glimpses of moorhens, herons, mallards and even a kingfisher. Half-way to Etal Castle the track leaves the river and heads across a wide open meadow lined by an ancient hawthorn hedge. A mile or so further and train, river and castle all meet up again. The final treat as you get off is to watch the driver and his mate shunt Lady Augusta onto a turntable, heave her through 180°, and back onto the track for the return trip.

Etal castle is run by English Heritage and can be either a large grassy play ground near the river for the under-5's or a fascinating lesson in Border History for those old enough to concentrate on the audio taped tour. It was crucially involved in the Battle of Flodden Field, four miles away, where in the space of two and a half hours the huge Scots army, led by King James IV was slaughtered and Scottish hopes of full independence were dashed. Now it is four walls and a few dark hiding places shared with the pigeons, although the indoor exhibition does also have some fine displays of armour and various weapons. Take the train back to Heatherslaw and take stock of energy levels and enthusiasm. It is worth the short walk across the curious steel bridge to the Heatherslaw Corn Mill: a 19th Century restored and working mill, complete with huge wooden water wheel and three large millstones working away at corn, barley and rye. There is an excellent hands-on children's trail, which starts by telling you about the grains and allowing the kids to do a bit of hand grinding. See how the oats for porridge are made and depending on your relative bent for cooking or eating, there are bags of flour or home-made cakes and biscuits to take home.

The mill machinery is all well-displayed for the technologically minded: endless cogs and wheels, shafts and brakes. Others can simply admire the huge water wheel turning slowly and watch grain pouring from giant wood hoppers down shoots and onto the mill wheels. There is even a mirror so you can see the grains disappearing under the grind stone.

Next to the mill is The Granary Tea Room, a very child-friendly cafe. The menu is simple but everything is home-made and served with a smile. The cakes are particularly irresistible. Toilets are at Heatherslaw on the mill side of the river, or in Etal village, there are none by the railway at either end.

Fact File

- ADDRESS Heatherslaw Railway, Ford Forge, Heatherslaw, Cornhill-on-Tweed, Northumberland
- TELEPHONE 01890 820244
- DIRECTIONS A1 towards Berwick, B6353 to Ford and B6354 to Heatherslaw
- PUBLIC TRANSPORT Buses from Morpeth or Berwick (summer Sundays only) (01670 533128)
- DISTANCE 65 miles
- TRAVEL TIME 1 hour 30 minutes
- OPENING 10.00am-5.00pm daily Easter to end October. Santa Specials in December
- PRICES £3.20 adults, £1.80 children, under-5's £1.00
- RESTAURANT FACILITIES At Corn Mill
- NAPPY CHANGING FACILITIES At Corn Mill
- HIGH CHAIRS Yes
- DOGS Yes
- PUSHCHAIR-FRIENDLY Yes
- NEARBY Chain Bridge Honey Farm, near Horncliffe, a working honey farm with an observation hive (01289 386362)

South Tynedale Railway

*Yes, I remember Adlestrop –
the name, because one afternoon
of heat the express-train drew up there
unwontedly. It was late June.*

YOU'LL REMEMBER GILDERDALE TOO, THE STOP ON THE SOUTH Tynedale Railway. Huffing and puffing its way under a bridge, the little train billows steam and shudders to a halt. "Where are we?" "Can we get off?" come the cries. We're in the middle of nowhere and yes they can. This is Gilderdale, just the name painted on a board and two seats on a bare platform – all around are green fields, a meandering river, tall trees and perfect peace. If you're looking for a child-sized train ride through glorious countryside then the South Tynedale Railway deep in the North Pennines is just the place.

> "Poke your noses into the engine shed where the locomotives are lovingly tended"

It consists of part of the old branch line between Haltwhistle and Alston, which closed in 1976 and re-opened in 1983, the Alston to Gilderdale section having been changed from standard to narrow gauge.

Alston Station boasts that it is the highest narrow gauge railway in the country (875' above sea-level) and certainly the approach to the town is spectacular. From every direction, roads roll across heather-clad moors, with hills and valleys stretching to the horizon. Striped snow markers alongside the dry-stone walls remind the city driver just how isolated this part of the country can be, and suggest that a weather check would be a good idea before setting off for a winter train ride (there can still be snow in May!)

There are five steam engines of which two are working. You can make the three-mile round trip between Alston and Gilderdale in 40 minutes, just about the right length to keep young travellers happy, looking out of the window at the cows and sheep or (if it is not too crowded) peering at the engine, heads in the smoky breeze, from the open end of the carriage. The train is staffed entirely by volunteers who are friendly and informative. They fielded some of our children's questions ("Why is the steam raining?") and at the Gilderdale stop they allowed the four-year-old to climb up next to the driver and pull the chain to make the train WHEESH! On a busy day this might not be possible, but it is worth asking.

You can walk back on a footpath alongside the railway line, but would need a backpack or sling as the path is too overgrown for a buggy. Back at Alston station a volunteer may take you up into the signal box to look at the row of polished levers and you can poke your noses into the engine shed where the locomotives are lovingly tended and restored.

The shop (also the ticket office) has plenty of Thomas the Tank paraphernalia, books and cards, while the tiny cafe sells home-made cakes and sandwiches. You have to sit outside but there is plenty to watch as the drivers shunt the engine to and fro and stoke up for the next trip. If a train is coming or going be sure to watch out for the signalman and the driver handing over the key token, a key in a black bag which opens the signal outside the station ensuring that only one train travels along the line at a time. More of a formality than a real safety measure here, but the idea of a special key as well as a whistle, a flag and a hat all add to the magical image of a train driver.

There are various special events during the year such as a Thomas the Tank Engine weekend, a Teddy Bear Day, and Santa Specials.

After the ride, walk up the hill into Alston, a pleasant town with steep cobbled streets, a market cross and arty-crafty shops. Look out for the special buns at Smileys Bakery on the right as you go up the hill, and take some Alston Fat Rascals or Stout Fellows home for tea. If you are picnicking there are some benches at the top of the town, beside a well-equipped children's play area. For a more substantial meal there numerous cafes and pubs, notably The Victoria Inn with a separate dining room and The Turk's Head Inn which offers a children's menu.

Fact File

- ADDRESS South Tynedale Railway, Alston, Cumbria
- TELEPHONE 01434 381696
- DIRECTIONS Take the A686 from Hexham. Signposted on roads into Alston
- PUBLIC TRANSPORT Bus services from Haltwhistle (not on Sundays), Newcastle, or Keswick
- DISTANCE 40 miles
- TRAVEL TIME 1 hour 20 minutes
- OPENING Weekends from Easter to end October, daily during Easter week, Whitsun half-term and summer school holidays. Trains run hourly from 11.15am-4.00pm
- PRICES Adults £2.50, children £1.00, under-5's free
- RESTAURANT FACILITIES In Alston
- NAPPY CHANGING FACILITIES Yes
- HIGH CHAIRS In Alston
- DOGS Yes
- PUSHCHAIR-FRIENDLY Yes
- NEARBY Alston is a pleasant town for a wander

Tanfield Railway

"ALL ABOARD, NEXT STOP CAUSEY ARCH!" THE GUARD SLAMS THE LAST carriage doors, waves his green flag and with a "whoo - whoo" the gleaming engine creeps away. Slowly, slowly at first, then there's a sudden "wheesh!", smoke billows, we jolt forwards in our seats and we're off! For steam railway enthusiasts and for kids Tanfield has all the right ingredients and grimy excitement to keep everyone happy.

You can board Tanfield Railway at four stops, Sunniside village, Andrews House (Tanfield), East Tanfield (from May 1997) or Causey Arch, and make the hour-long round trip. To make a day of it you should have a look at the Marley Hill Engine Shed at Andrews House and take a walk in the gorge below Causey Arch too. Start at Andrews House and go to the Shed first, then take the train to Sunniside and back down again, alighting at Causey Arch and catching a later train back.

The railway is the oldest line in the world, built in the early 18th century to carry coal from Tanfield Pit down to the ships on the River Tyne. The three miles of restored track offer a varied journey, passing from suburban Sunniside to an open valley and then entering Causey Woods with glimpses of the spectacular arch through the trees. You travel in style in coaches dating from the 1880's and can choose between a saloon carriage with space for kids to roam up and down and an open-air platform at either end, or an individual compartment with its own doors to slam and ancient windows to lower down on cord.

"An individual compartment with its own doors to slam and ancient windows to lower down on cord"

Kids love the hustle and bustle of it all: the flag, the whistle blowing, the guard pacing up and down in his cap. They also love the dirt: ours watched in amazement as the two drivers shovelled coal into the furnace then clambered onto the engine to fill the water tank, hands and faces streaked with black, boots grey and sodden. It's all so much grimier and noisier than the sanitised world of Thomas the Tank Engine, whose driver has never even the smallest speck of soot on his nose!

The Marley Hill Shed has been a working shed since 1854 and has plenty of activity still going on. Bring your wellies as there is a fair bit of oil and coal dust underfoot. You can wander beside the huge locos and carriages and admire the original tools that are used in the restoration. The toilets here are the only ones at the railway.

After the Shed, walk down to Andrews House station to buy your tickets. There's a small shop with cards and gifts, and a cafe selling snacks, but nothing substantial enough for lunch, so if you're making a day of it bring your own picnic. There are plenty of pleasant spots down in the gorge beside Causey Arch, the next stop down the line.

Causey Arch is the world's oldest surviving railway bridge, built in 1725 as part of the wagon way from the nearby colliery to the River

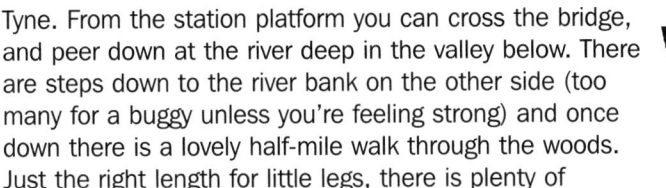

Tyne. From the station platform you can cross the bridge, and peer down at the river deep in the valley below. There are steps down to the river bank on the other side (too many for a buggy unless you're feeling strong) and once down there is a lovely half-mile walk through the woods. Just the right length for little legs, there is plenty of entertainment along the way with wild flowers, wild raspberries and blackberries and several wooden bridges criss-crossing the river. At the far end the path takes you steeply back up hill and it's a short walk along the line back to the station. There is a car park at Causey Arch too.

Look out for the special events such as Teddy Bear Day, Big Engine Weekend, and Children's Weekend. At Christmas there are Santa steamings, you need to book ahead for these though as no tickets are issued on the day.

Fact File

- ADDRESS Tanfield Railway, Sunniside, Gateshead, Tyne & Wear
- TELEPHONE 0191 274 2002
- DIRECTIONS Just off the A6076 Sunniside to Stanley Road
- PUBLIC TRANSPORT X30 bus stops at the entrance on weekdays, buses 706, 708 and M44 to Sunniside on Sundays
- DISTANCE 8 miles
- TRAVEL TIME 20 minutes
- OPENING Sundays 11.00am-4.00pm (summer) and to 3.15pm (winter). Also Thursdays in the summer holidays, Easter long weekend and Bank Holiday Mondays
- PRICES £3.30 adults, £1.70 children, under-5's free
- RESTAURANT FACILITIES Limited
- NAPPY CHANGING FACILITIES No
- HIGH CHAIRS No
- DOGS Yes
- PUSHCHAIR-FRIENDLY Yes
- NEARBY Gibside Chapel, Burnopfield, a National Trust property with lovely walks (01207 542255)

The Sun Has Got His Hat On

Allen Banks & Plankey Mill

A WOODLAND WALK, A CHANCE TO PADDLE IN THE COOL RIVER ALLEN and a grassy spot to lie in the sun and gaze up at the blue sky – what more could anyone want on a lazy summer's afternoon? Allen Banks and Plankey Mill are two picnic spots at either end of a stretch of National Trust land along the Allen valley a few miles west of Haydon Bridge. The land which links them has enough to keep young children busy all day while parents (when they're not wading in the river grasping a determined toddler's hand or chasing after a couple of young explorers amongst the trees) can enjoy the peace of the woods and the beauty of the water.

> "An area of flat rock worn into grooves and smooth channels just great for paddling"

If you park at Allen Banks, at the northern end, there is a pleasant grassy area just near the car park, where you can picnic and bat a ball around. When you're ready to set off there are three different walks on offer. The shortest is the Bridge Walk which takes about half an hour, following the path alongside the river then climbing a steep flight of wooden steps up the hillside and continuing along the edge of the Ridley Estate to the right. You are walking beneath mighty deciduous trees, mature beech, oak, sycamore and chestnut while the path is edged with mosses and ferns, wild garlic, wild raspberries and blackberries according to the season. After a while the path drops down again to the river and you emerge at a small suspension bridge, across here there is an area of flat rock worn into grooves and smooth channels just great for paddling. If you walk back on this side the path passes through open fields, full of cows grazing. Alternatively if you're feeling energetic and can carry anybody who is too small for another steep flight of steps, you can set off on the Morralee Wood Walk.

This is a circular walk of about half an hour and takes you to a tarn set amongst larch and Scots pine trees where white water lilies bloom in the summer. Carrying on along the river on the third walk, the Riverside Walk, you come to a large open area below Raven Crag. Here you'll find 'The Bathing Pool', a cool deep pool in the river where you can swim, children can splash in the shallows and there's plenty of space for picnicking too.

Continue on for another twenty minutes or so and you will come to Plankey Mill. This is the southern end where there's a much larger car park, a second suspension bridge, a small beach area and a large field where you can shake out the rug and spread yourselves around. There are toilets in the car parks but no other facilities, so bring everything with you. You can push a buggy through the woods but it would be a struggle negotiating all the tree roots and stumps, much easier to bring a sling or backpack if you have one.

Fact File

- ADDRESS Allen Banks, Hexham, Northumberland
- TELEPHONE None
- DIRECTIONS A69 to a few miles beyond Haydon Bridge. Turn towards Ridley College and follow signs to Allenbanks
- PUBLIC TRANSPORT Bus 685 Newcastle to Carlisle stops within walking distance (01434 602061)
- DISTANCE 30 miles
- TRAVEL TIME 45 minutes
- OPENING Anytime
- PRICES Free
- RESTAURANT FACILITIES No
- NAPPY CHANGING FACILITIES No
- HIGH CHAIRS No
- DOGS Yes
- PUSHCHAIR-FRIENDLY No
- NEARBY Hadrian's Wall, Vindolanda Fort and Museum (01434 344277)

Bolam Lake

There is nothing – absolutely nothing – half so much worth doing as simply messing about in boats

ON A HOT STILL SUMMER'S DAY WHAT COULD BE MORE PLEASANT THAN drifting about in a boat, hands trailing in the water, fishing nets dipping in and out for tiddlers? Bolam Lake is a perfect place for pottering about with kids in a little inflatable boat (bring your own), playing ambushing games in the woods or simply unrolling a rug and opening a picnic basket. A man-made lake created from the marshes of Bolam Bog in the nineteenth century, it is now a country park run by Northumberland County Council.

There are three car parks, one on the corner nearest to Belsay, one at the west end which is only about five minutes walk from the main picnic area and the third at the north eastern end which is the only one with toilets and is also near the Visitor centre and the ice cream kiosk, both of which are open at busy times (weekends and summer holidays).

"Three wooden jetties where you can sit by the water watching the damselflies hovering"

The lake is set in varied woodland and although close to the road, the path that takes you round the lake twists and winds amongst the trees so that you feel you're in the heart of the woods. There are plenty of overhanging branches to swing from and logs to clamber over and in one favourite spot there is a hollow tree that small people can climb inside. Be prepared to play owls and fat teddy bears for a while before opening your sandwiches. Every so often the path opens onto the lake's edge and there's a glimpse of the water and the birds. There are three wooden jetties where you can sit by the water watching the damselflies hovering and the water boatmen skating over the surface.

The west end of the lake is still marshy with reedbeds and between the car park and the Pheasant Field picnic area the woodland path becomes a boardwalk. Our children seem to enjoy tramping along this peering at the mud on either side and it allows for some easy buggy pushing. The west end of the lake is a nature sanctuary and boating and fishing are not allowed. The field has a number of picnic tables and shady trees to set up camp under. There is enough space for games too; last time we went cricket, badminton, frisbee and at least three different games of football were going on. Outside the school holidays it can be blissfully peaceful, with only the birds for company.

The stretch between the field and the Visitor centre has a shallow beach-like area which is probably the best spot to launch your boat from if you have one and feel like going for a row. This is a popular place and can get a bit crowded on a hot day. Children can paddle but it would be wise to wear shoes as notices warn of broken glass. The lake is not suitable for swimming (although people do), as water from the surrounding farmland drains into it. The bottom is also very muddy and in some spots the mud is deeper than it looks.

The lake has a number of ducks and moorhens and a flock of swans. Be warned if you visit in springtime when the cygnets are small, the swans can be quite fierce. If you're there on a quiet day you may well see other birds in the woods and there are roe deer. In winter small birds such as marsh tits and coal tits will come to the car parks and if you're lucky may be tame enough to feed from your hand. The Visitor Centre has books, maps and gifts for sale and is staffed by countryside officers. Throughout the summer holidays and on some weekends there is a kiosk next to it selling ice creams and cold drinks.

If you feel like a more energetic walk, drive on west from Bolam Lake for nearly a mile and then do the half-hour walk up to Shaftoe Crags on the right hand side of the road. You'll need a backpack rather than a pushchair here. There is a cafe, The Stable Coffee Shop in Bolam West Houses, where you can have a cup of tea and delicious home-made cake, when you come down again.

Fact File

- ADDRESS Bolam Lake Country Park, Belsay, Northumberland
- TELEPHONE 01661 881234
- DIRECTIONS A696 from Newcastle to Belsay, follow signs to Bolam Lake
- PUBLIC TRANSPORT No. 508 bus from Haymarket or Gateshead, summer Sundays only (01670 533128)
- DISTANCE 18 miles
- TRAVEL TIME 40 minutes
- OPENING Anytime
- PRICES Free
- RESTAURANT FACILITIES Nearby
- NAPPY CHANGING FACILITIES No
- HIGH CHAIRS No
- DOGS Yes
- PUSHCHAIR-FRIENDLY Yes
- NEARBY Newcastle Airport for rooftop spectators' gallery (0191 286 0966)

Bowlees

FEELING IN NEED OF SOME PEACE AND QUIET – THE ROAR OF A waterfall instead of traffic, trees instead of houses arching over your head? Come to Bowlees and recharge your batteries in this tranquil little valley. All you will need are your sarnies, a rug and a few pairs of wellies (spare trousers too if your kids have the same magnetic attraction for water as ours do).

Bowlees is a sheltered picnic area beside the river just beyond Middleton-in-Teesdale. There are four waterfalls and a delightful half-mile walk through the woods to another fall at Gibsons Cave. A quarter of a mile across the fields there is the impressive Low Force waterfall and a short car ride further up the road will bring you to High Force, the highest and most dramatic of the River Tees waterfalls.

Bowlees is well-signposted and there is ample car parking just off the road. There are some rather basic toilets in the car park. Just beyond them there is a stretch of half-built dry stone wall with a display board about the technique and an invitation to have a go. Watch your toes with toddlers lugging heavy stones around, but this can be fun for older children. A little further on, the trees open out and you come to a large grassy area, just the place to spread out the rug. You can get right down to the water's edge here, below one of the waterfalls. It is shallow and a great place for older kids to paddle and potter. Younger ones can play on the bank where there are some fabulous trees with spreading branches, just right for tunnelling into and making a den. There is also a steep hillock to climb and run down.

When you're ready to stretch your legs follow the path up the steps (difficult for buggies) and along the path to Gibsons cave. The land is all part of the Raby Castle estate

> "Some fabulous trees with spreading branches, just right for tunnelling into and making a den"

but the route to the fall is open to the public. It is an easy stroll, much enlivened when we were there by enormous numbers of ladybirds sitting on the fence at the side of the path. The cave is only a large hollow where you can stand to watch the waterfall, but the fall itself, Summerhill Force, is impressive.

Return the way you came and cross the bridge by the car park to reach the Visitor Centre in an old Methodist Chapel. This is open 10.30am-4.30pm from Easter to the end of October and has natural history displays on the geology, plant and wildlife of the Upper Teesdale. There are models, pictures, photos and rocks to look at and also cards and books for sale. There is a small entrance fee.

Turn left from the centre and cross the road to find the footpath down to Low Force. The falls are tremendous: here the river tumbles over shelving rocks as if down a flight of steps, falling into a seething pool below, like "bubbling coca-cola" as my daughter put it. The children will also enjoy the wobbly bridge they must cross over on the way.

If everyone's game for another waterfall you can return to the car and drive on a little further to High Force. There is a parking charge of about £1.00 and a small admission charge for the fall (50p adults, 25p children) and it is half a mile along the path to the waterfall. The path is gravelled but wide enough for a pushchair. Again it is a pleasant woodland walk and the fall itself is spectacular. Thundering 70' down over huge rocks, High Force is England's largest waterfall. The roaring of the water, the spray and the writhing foam in the pool below make it an awe-inspiring sight. Back at the car park there is a hotel serving bar meals and teas – children are welcome – or you can return to Middleton-in-Teesdale where there are several pubs.

Fact File

- ADDRESS Bowlees, Middleton-in-Teesdale, County Durham
- TELEPHONE 01833 622292 (Visitor centre)
- DIRECTIONS A1 south, exit on the A688 to Staindrop, then the B6279 to Eggleston, and the B6282 to Middleton-in-Teesdale. B6277 to Bowlees
- PUBLIC TRANSPORT Bus from Darlington on Sundays
- DISTANCE 58 miles
- TRAVEL TIME 1 hour 15 minutes
- OPENING All times
- PRICES Free (mostly)
- RESTAURANT FACILITIES No
- NAPPY CHANGING FACILITIES No
- HIGH CHAIRS No
- DOGS Yes
- PUSHCHAIR-FRIENDLY No
- NEARBY Raby Castle, a Medieval castle with 200-acre deer park, carriage collection, walled garden and fine paintings (01833 660202)

Dunstanburgh

RISING A HUNDRED FEET ABOVE THE SHORE AND CROWNING magnificent basaltic cliffs, Dunstanburgh Castle is one of the most imposing fortresses in Northumberland. On the north and east the sea dashes against the rocks, and the wind and spray of countless winter storms have weathered the castle walls. There are many spectacular castles in Northumberland, but Dunstanburgh stands alone. Overlooking the surf in solitary splendour, far from the villages of Embleton and Craster, the only way to reach it is on foot. Bitingly cold in winter, yet stunning on a clear day, there can be few such romantic or dramatic picnic spots. Few places as windy too, so when you visit do come prepared to wrap up warmly.

You can approach it from north or south, the castle is well-signposted in both directions. From Embleton you take a right turn towards the coast and can park along the road to the golf course. There is a path alongside the links or you can cut across and walk along the beach. Embleton Bay is a glorious two-mile stretch of sand with shallow rock pools and dunes, perfect for picnicking with children.

> **"Walk down to the sea from a flight of steps and a gateway in the castle wall"**

It's also a great place for beachcombing. If your kids enjoy foraging for treasures, keep a sharp eye out for quartz crystals, which come from the cove beneath the castle.

The inner and the coastal paths converge at the cove below the castle. The rocks here are quite a sight. On the shore at low tide you will see Saddle Rock, a limestone causeway leading into the water. Further round, the rock has formed into distinct columns. The precipitous cliffs are known as Gull Crag and are a nesting ground for a huge colony of sea birds, whom you will hear long before you see them. In a storm, the sea rushes up the famous hollow chasm in the headland, known as Rumble Churn, with a great rumbling noise and water and foam spout out the top.

The entrance to the castle is on the far side. The castle was built in the 14th century and has had a chequered history passing through the hands of various noble families. A stronghold of the Red Rose of Northumberland during the wars of the Roses, it was much damaged during sieges. After the 16th century it was never repaired and has stood in ruins ever since.

The main buildings left are the entrance gateway with two semi-circular towers, one of which can still be climbed. Keep a very close eye on small children as there is only basic fencing between the stairs and a sheer drop in some places. On the west side, the Lilburn Tower with walls six-feet thick, still stands strong and forbidding. In between there are old walls and foundations and a fair bit of exploring and scrambling around to do. You can walk down to the sea from a flight of steps and a gateway in the castle wall leading down to a deep cove. As you stand watching the waves batter the rocks and the stones crash together it is easy to understand why it was such a brilliant site for a fortress.

You can approach the castle from Craster too and if you don't want to go via the beach this is the preferred option. The village car park is on the right as you drive in, with toilets and a cafe right beside it. It is a short walk to the coastal path and then a mile and a half up to the castle. It is a more open path, not being hemmed in by golfing greens or flying golf balls, and it is possible to push a buggy along. You walk through fields shared with cows and sheep, while flocks of gulls, oyster catchers and eider chatter away in the rocks beside you.

Fact File

- ADDRESS Dunstanburgh Castle, Craster, Alnwick, Northumberland
- TELEPHONE 01665 576231
- DIRECTIONS A1 to Alnwick, B1340 to Craster
- PUBLIC TRANSPORT Northumbria bus 501 from Alnwick to Berwick stops at Craster. Connections from Newcastle
- DISTANCE 32 miles
- TRAVEL TIME 50 minutes
- OPENING Daily April to October 10.00am-6.00pm (4.00pm in October). 10.00am-4.00pm Wednesday-Sunday the rest of the year
- PRICES Adults £1.60, children 80p. Under-5's, English Heritage and National Trust members free
- RESTAURANT FACILITIES No
- NAPPY CHANGING FACILITIES No
- HIGH CHAIRS No
- DOGS Yes
- PUSHCHAIR-FRIENDLY No
- NEARBY Craster village for pub and teashop, and kippers for sale. Howick Hall Gardens (01665 577285) for walks in formal gardens

Finchale Priory

Bare ruin'd choirs, where late the sweet birds sang

ON A LONG HOT SUMMER'S DAY TAKE A PICNIC TO FINCHALE PRIORY. Spread out the blanket amongst the ruined cloisters or sit under the shady trees beside the old hall. The children can burn off some energy exploring and then flop on the slopes beside the river. The priory stands in a wonderful spot on a bend in the Wear so you can picnic and play amongst the ruins first then cross the footbridge and walk in the woods or paddle and fish in the river.

Finchale was built in three stages between the 12th and 16th centuries and each period has left architectural remains. You can get a feel for the buildings as you wander amongst the crumbling walls. There is some fine tracery in the arches of the old choir and a line of arcades almost intact along the side of the nave. St Godric's tomb – cut from a huge block of stone – is still in the chapel, the cover slab is gone but you can still see the grooves in the stone where it was once fastened on. While you walk and dream about the order and the peace there must have been once when monks came here from Durham for their holidays, your little darlings will be enjoying the place in their own way.

> "A wonderful spot on a bend in the Wear where you can picnic and play amongst the ruins"

The small rooms, crumbly stairs and lines of arches are perfect for chasing through, hiding and jumping out. Our crew were delighted to discover a "dungeon" and boasted to each other of the dastardly deeds that once went on there. It is actually a vaulted cellar below the refectory, but who needs to know that?

Since the priory is fairly compact and well-fenced older children can be given free rein for exploring. Younger ones need to be watched though as there are several sets of steps leading up to sheer drops and other steps leading down which appear in the path without warning. The succession of rooms can be confusing to children too, since one stone wall looks much like another.

☞   There is a small shop selling sweets and ices outside the gate to the priory. You can also buy food to feed the goats who amble around in the car park, though they seem to manage pretty well on the remains of picnics and are obviously well-used to foraging in the bins. Toilets are limited; there is a portakabin just beyond the car park entrance and there is occasionally a ladies toilet open in the building behind the shop.

You can clamber down to the river from the car park or if you cross the bridge and walk a couple of hundred yards along the path there are a number of silty beaches and flat stones from which kids can paddle. It's worth bringing a fishing net as there are plenty of tiddlers. It's too shallow for swimming but come prepared with spare clothes as the river bottom is rather slimy and if you don't someone is bound to fall in.

Fact File

- ADDRESS Finchale Priory, Durham, County Durham
- TELEPHONE 0191 386 3828
- DIRECTIONS A1(M) south, exiting Chester-le-Street and taking the A167. Follow signs, the Priory is on a minor road off the A167
- PUBLIC TRANSPORT Buses from Durham to Cocken Lodge or Brasside (0191 384 3720)
- DISTANCE 15 miles
- TRAVEL TIME 25 minutes
- OPENING Daily 12 noon-5.00pm from April to September
- PRICES Adults £1.00, children 50p, under-5's and English Heritage members free
- RESTAURANT FACILITIES No
- NAPPY CHANGING FACILITIES No
- HIGH CHAIRS No
- DOGS Yes
- PUSHCHAIR-FRIENDLY Yes
- NEARBY Durham city castle, cathedral, shops, museums and Botanical gardens

Other Books IN THE SERIES

ALSO AVAILABLE IN THIS SERIES:
The Heinz Guide to
DAYS OUT WITH KIDS
in the **North West**
TRIED-AND-TESTED FUN FAMILY OUTINGS IN LANCASHIRE, MERSEYSIDE, DERBYSHIRE AND CHESHIRE.
128 PAGES, PAPERBACK, £4.99

The Heinz Guide to
DAYS OUT WITH KIDS
in the **Heart of England**
TRIED-AND-TESTED FUN FAMILY OUTINGS IN WARWICKSHIRE, WORCESTERSHIRE, SHROPSHIRE, GLOUCESTERSHIRE, STAFFORDSHIRE, LEICESTERSHIRE, AND WEST MIDLANDS.
128 PAGES, PAPERBACK, £4.99

The Heinz Guide to
DAYS OUT WITH KIDS
in the **South East**
TRIED-AND-TESTED FUN FAMILY OUTINGS IN KENT, SUSSEX, SURREY, HAMPSHIRE, BERKSHIRE, ESSEX, HERTFORDSHIRE, BEDFORDSHIRE AND BUCKINGHAMSHIRE.
168 PAGES, PAPERBACK, £5.99

ALL OTHER BOOKS IN THE SERIES ARE AVAILABLE FROM:

The Heinz Guide to DAYS OUT WITH KIDS
BON•BON VENTURES
24 ENDLESHAM ROAD
LONDON SW12 8JU
TEL: 0181 488 3011
FAX: 0181 265 1700

PAYMENT MAY BE MADE BY CHEQUE OR POSTAL ORDER PAYABLE TO BONBON VENTURES.
PLEASE ALLOW £1.00 POSTAGE AND PACKING FOR THE FIRST BOOK, AND 50P PER BOOK FOR SUBSEQUENT BOOKS.

Be a winner with

Heinz

Heinz celebrated 100 years of the famous "57 Varieties" advertising slogan in 1996 and produced this valuable limited edition boxed set of products to mark the occasion. Each product is made to an original recipe, recently uncovered by company archivists, and the cans feature labels from the early part of the century.

We have five boxed sets to give away to *Heinz Guide to Days Out with Kids* readers. All you have to do is write on a postcard to the address below, telling us how many Heinz varieties you think there are in the UK today:

a) **57**
b) **190**
c) **360**

Entries must arrive by August 31 1997. The first five correct entries picked at random will win a boxed set.

> HEINZ GUIDE COMPETITION
> PO BOX 57
> DISS
> NORFOLK 1P22 3BB